LOWE'S
Let's Build Something Together

creative
ideas
for home and garden®
MAKEOVERS

LOWE'S COMPANIES, INC.

Robert Niblock, PRESIDENT, CEO,
AND CHAIRMAN OF THE BOARD

Melissa S. Birdsong, DIRECTOR, TREND
AND DESIGN

Mary Carpenter, MERCHANDISE DIRECTOR

Bob Gfeller, SENIOR VP, MARKETING

Carol Knuth, VP, MERCHANDISING

Mike Menser, SENIOR VP, GENERAL
MERCHANDISE MANAGER

Larry D. Stone, SENIOR EXECUTIVE VP,
MERCHANDISING AND MARKETING

Sandy Culver, CUSTOMER RELATIONSHIP
MANAGER

Anne Serafin, MERCHANDISING DIRECTOR

LOWE'S CREATIVE IDEAS FOR MAKEOVERS

René Klein, PROJECT DIRECTOR FOR LOWE'S
CUSTOM BOOKS, SUNSET PUBLISHING
CORPORATION

Stephanie Patton, DIRECTOR, SPC CUSTOM
PUBLISHING

Shane Jordan, ACCOUNT MANAGER,
SPC CUSTOM PUBLISHING

Sally W. Smith, EDITOR

Lisa Stockwell, WRITER

Alice Lankford Elmore and Kelly Margaret Smith,
CONSULTING EDITORS

Gary Hespenheide, ART DIRECTOR

Randy Miyake, ILLUSTRATOR

John Edmonds, COPY EDITOR

Sheryl Jones and Ryan Kelly, PRODUCTION EDITORS

Nanette Cardon, INDEXER

Cover: This kitchen, designed for enthusiastic cooks who love to entertain, matches the cool, industrial ambience of stainless-steel appliances with the warm tones of cherry and birch cabinetry. See pages 20–21 for the story.

Photograph: Bryan Johnson

Page 1: This bathroom was showing its age. A makeover gave it crisp, charming cottage style (see pages 98–99).

Right: See pages 50–51 for the details on this updated dining area.

10 9 8 7 6 5 4 3 2 1

First Printing April 2006

Copyright © 2006 Sunset Publishing Corporation, Menlo Park, California 94025. First edition. All rights reserved, including the right of reproduction in whole or in part in any form.

Library of Congress Control Number: 2006922998

ISBN-13: 978-0-376-00925-8
ISBN-10: 0-376-00925-X

Printed in the United States

PHOTO CREDITS

Left (L), Right (R), Top (T), Middle (M), Bottom (B)

Jean Allsopp: 70, 76; Robbie Caponetto: 6BL, 8R, 9, 16B, 17, 30M, B, 31, 34BL, 62B, 63, 100M, 101; ClosetMaid: 82ML, MR, BL, BR; Gary Conaughton: 54B; Laurey W. Glenn: 6BR, 7B, 26M, B, 27, 28, 56TR, B, 57, 60TR, MR, BL, BR, 68, 72, 73, 81 T, M, 92B, 93, 106B, 120M, T, BL, BR, 121; Jay Graham: 95BR; Margot Hartford: 77; Jon Jensen: 55B; Bryan Johnson: 10, 12M, 13, 14B, 15TM,TR, B, 20, 29ML, BL, 34BR, 35, 53MR, 88, 89, 94, 95TR, 104, 105, 125ML; Muffy Kibbey: 48B; David Duncan Livingston: 95L; Peter Malinowski/Insite: 33B; Sylvia Martin: 69; E. Andrew McKinney: 79BL, BR, 80; John O'Hagan: 6T, 7T, 19TR, 22M, BR, BL, 23, 24B, 25, 34TR, 36B, 37, 40M, 41, 44, 46BL, BR, 47, 49TR, B, 50M, 52T, B, 53ML, 58ML, BL, M59, 61, 64M, 65, 66, 67, 74, 75, 78, 84, 90TR, BL, BR, 91, 98B, 99, 102B, 103, 107L, BR, 108M, 109, 110M, 111, 114, 115, 116, 117, 118TR, 118M, 122R, 125MR; John O'Hagan and Jason Wallis: 97; Bradley Olman: 19BR; David Papazian: 32L, R; Lisa Romerein: 38M, 39; Brian Vanden Brink: 96; Jason Wallis: 112, 124

bring your ideas to life ...

Your home is not only your personal haven, but an expression of who you are and how you live. If you don't love the spaces you inhabit every day, it may be time for a makeover. And if you are **ready to remodel** and don't know exactly where to start, you've come to the right place for inspiration!

Transforming a room is both *exciting* and challenging. To help you get started, we've put together a gallery of remodels, from kitchens to garages. Our makeovers, ranging from budget-wise solutions to sky's-the-limit transformations, offer lots of ideas and advice for turning ho-hum spaces into **rooms you'll love**.

You will also find helpful hints on how to *improve* your lighting, maximize storage, save on energy bills, and make your home more accessible, as well as **projects** you can build yourself.

Finally, we welcome you back to our Lowe's Creative Ideas book series, which includes *Lowe's Creative Ideas for Organizing Your Home* and *Lowe's Creative Ideas for Kids' Spaces*. All of our books can be purchased at your local Lowe's store and online at Lowes.com, along with books from our other series, including the new edition of *Lowe's Complete Home Improvement and Repair*. They are all filled with the same **practical information** you'll find in our *Creative Ideas for Home and Garden*® magazine.

Melissa

Melissa Birdsong
Director, Trend and Design
Lowe's Companies, Inc.

12

contents

61

78

114

107

the magic of
makeovers

IT'S EXCITING TO LAUNCH A MAKEOVER. What a thrill to create a dream master bedroom suite, a truly functional kitchen, a room your kids will love!

This book is designed to inspire you as you start turning idle musings into firm decisions. On the following pages, you'll find examples of exciting transformations, room by room. Some makeovers are truly simple—just the addition of new color or fabric. Others strip back a room to bare walls and floors and start anew. Whatever their scale, they all offer creative ideas

These examples provide everything you need to get your own remodeling ideas flowing. Let them inspire you, and then come to Lowe's. We can't make your decisions for you, but we are here to help at every stage of the process with advice, materials, and installation.

Each of the rooms shown here is the successful result of a real-life makeover. For additional photos and information, see pages 22–23 (kitchen), 46 (entry), 62–63 (home office), 72–73 (bedroom), and 92–93 (bathroom).

A CREATIVE ADVENTURE Any remodeling project begins with idea gathering, and that's what this book is all about. We've filled these pages with more than 50 different makeovers featuring the latest trends in color, design, and function. The projects here are geared to the way people live today. Our kitchens all provide for both food preparation and convivial gathering, while our master bathrooms reflect the trend to more spa-like retreats. Because most homeowners now prefer a casual lifestyle, family rooms prevail over formal dining and living rooms.

Each chapter focuses on a separate room of the house, and each makeover offers ideas for maximizing space, increasing usability, and evoking your own personal style. Many are accompanied by floor plans that help you see how the solutions improved the space. Tips throughout the book highlight information you can use. You'll also see many products, from major appliances to nifty storage items, that can provide the perfect touch for your makeover.

Throughout the book you'll find easy projects you can do yourself, as well as special features on ways to make your home more enjoyable—from improved lighting and more efficient appliances to great storage solutions.

With ideas gathered from these real-life makeovers, come into Lowe's. Our employees can help you get started creating a space you will love.

LOWE'S CAN HELP

As you embark on a makeover, let Lowe's and Lowes.com help you. Look to us for the following services and assistance:

- Kitchen and bathroom design and planning
- Appliance selection
- Window and door selection
- Color consultation
- In-store how-to clinics
- Online tutorials
- Special-order products
- Installation facilitation
- Delivery

Consider having Lowe's do installation for you. Our services include countertops, cabinetry, appliances, flooring, and doors and windows. All the work is guaranteed.

FROM DOWDY TO DRAMATIC A makeover can transform an outdated bathroom or kitchen into an up-to-date marvel. For the details on these now-beautiful rooms, see pages 100–101 for the bathroom and pages 16–17 for the kitchen.

kitchens

A KITCHEN IS ONE OF THE MOST SATISFYING

rooms to make over. Imagine improving the efficiency of the layout, creating convenient and abundant storage, or turning a cramped room into an open place where family members and friends will love to gather.

The key to a successful kitchen remodel is to determine your highest priorities—and never sacrifice them. For instance, if you're an avid cook, plan to spend on the appliances and workstations that make preparing meals a pleasure. If your focus is more on time with your family, save on the appliances and add an island where the kids can hang out.

The kitchens here range from low-cost successes to truly luxurious makeovers. In each category, there are lots of exciting ideas for creating a satisfying new kitchen.

FREE KITCHEN RENOVATION PLANNER

This unique guidebook has everything necessary to help you finalize the plans for your new kitchen. Order it by calling 1-877-777-1545, or online at Lowes.com/KitchenPlanner.

A kitchenette in a commercial building became an open-plan kitchen that's perfect for entertaining. For more information, see pages 20–21.

1

IN A TOTAL, SKY'S-THE-LIMIT MAKEOVER, you can do almost anything:

take out a wall here, add another there, relocate plumbing, rewire the electrical system. Here, five great remodels show how you can create the perfect kitchen when you can change whatever is necessary.

BEFORE Having outgrown their old kitchen, these homeowners envisioned a larger space that was both casual enough for the kids to hang out with friends in and elegant enough for large gatherings and intimate dinner parties. A poorly used den adjacent to the kitchen provided the perfect solution.

BEFORE

den

AFTER

AFTER Two rooms became one. By removing the wall between the kitchen and den, the homeowners not only created a more functional space but also integrated an attractive dining area and hospitality center into the plan. They followed a popular trend of mixing colors and finishes for visual interest. Choosing rich brown mouldings and countertops to balance the soft blue walls and light bisque cabinetry, they created an effect that is soothing yet cheerful. A tumbled stone backsplash in shades of brown pulls the color scheme together.

▲ **COOKING ISLAND** With lots of counter space to the front and sides of the cooktop, the island offers ample room for serving and casual dining above and easy access to pots and pans below.

▲ **EASY-GRIP KNOBS** Adding a distinctive touch to the kitchen's style, oversized taupe knobs featuring a cloisonné design make opening cabinet doors and drawers easy.

◀ **HOSPITALITY CENTER** In a corner of the new dining area, a hospitality center includes a refrigerator and ice-maker for entertaining large groups. The chocolate-colored marble tile backsplash, which contrasts with the bone-colored solid-surface countertop, adds elegance to this space.

BEFORE These empty-nesters wanted a sophisticated space where they could prepare gourmet meals together and entertain their friends. They envisioned a country look with warm colors and rustic features. Rearranging the existing space made the most sense. They felt they could maintain the same basic floor plan as long as they moved some appliances to create a better work triangle (see page 29) and capture unused space for increased storage.

▼ Open shelving in small niches on each side of the cooktop keeps oils and spices handy. Space beneath the staircase houses a wine chiller and other storage.

AFTER A French country décor was the theme for this makeover. Ginger-glazed wood cabinetry, rustic hardware, a warm gold granite countertop, and a deep porcelain sink provide the architectural details that set the style. A grand cooking center is the focal point for the new kitchen; with the cooktop situated there, the island can accommodate a comfortable, casual eating area as well as a prep sink. For easier access, the dishwasher to the left of the porcelain sink was raised.

FOCUS ON COOKING Moving the pantry to a closet made room for a professional-style cooking center on the wall beneath the stairway. Its backsplash, composed of 2-inch-square tumbled-marble tiles and a decorative tile border, is an attractive highlight. Not only is there adequate counter space on each side of the range, but large drawers keep utensils, pots, and pans within easy reach.

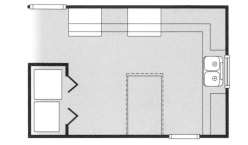

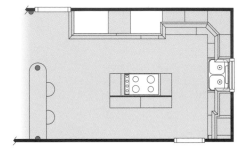

BEFORE The existing floor plan of this kitchen was full of challenges. Traffic flow was awkward, and the homeowners needed more space for storage, food preparation, and entertaining. A washer and dryer behind bifold doors in a closet created annoying background noise.

AFTER Thanks to a relocated laundry closet, the kitchen-dining area is now visible from the living room, so looks matter. Cherry cabinetry, with a rich chocolate glaze, adds traditional warmth to the open layout. Above the cabinets, stacked crown moulding provides definition and visually heightens the kitchen. Classic columns enhance that effect. Stone-like ceramic tile floors and a backsplash of 2-inch tumbled marble tile add extra elements of texture and contrast.

ROOM FOR EVERYONE The makeover increased storage and counter space along the walls and also allowed the homeowners to add a cooking island and breakfast bar. The island has extra storage and room for multiple cooks to prepare food. All work areas are well lit with functional recessed task lighting as well as matching pendants above the breakfast bar.

counterpoints

After cabinetry, work surfaces are probably the most noticeable elements of a kitchen. Certainly these heavily used countertops need to function well. Fortunately they can also be beautiful, given the wonderful array of materials in varying styles. Feel free to mix several different ones, taking into account the characteristics of each and the function it must serve. For instance, choose moisture-resistant solid surface around the sink and heat-resistant quartz or granite near the stove, with decorative ceramic tile as a backsplash. The following information will help you make your selection.

COUNTER HEIGHT

The average height for kitchen and bath counters ranges from 28 to 36 inches. For special circumstances, consider the following:
- For taller adults, 36 inches is more comfortable.
- Desktops are generally 28 inches high.
- For people in nonadjustable wheelchairs, the best range is 28 to 32 inches, depending on the function of the counter, and usable counter depth is 16 inches. Leave the area beneath a counter unobstructed for wheelchair access.

Granite

One of the hardest natural stone surfaces. Variegated patterns and color nuances in polished, glossy, or honed finishes. Variety of edging options. Durable. Moisture, scratch, and heat resistant, stain resistant if sealed. Use with drop-in or under-mounted sinks. Can be placed anywhere. $$$

Quartz

Luxurious surface made up of quartz crystals that absorb and reflect light. Variety of edging options. Durable. Moisture, stain, scratch, heat, and chip resistant; no need for sealing. Safe for food preparation. Use with drop-in or under-mounted sinks. Good in any location. $$$

Solid Surface

Nonporous manufactured product that can be molded to any shape you wish. Comes in a variety of colors and finishes; offers many edging options. Durable. Stain and moisture resistant. Virtually seamless, easy to clean. Can scratch or burn, so it needs protection against hot pots and knives. Consistent color throughout, so some stains and scratches can be buffed away. Sink can be integrated into countertop, or use drop-in or under-mounted sink. Use anywhere. $$

EDGING OPTIONS Each counter material offers various edge profiles, so you can choose what best suits the style of your kitchen. Rounded or straight edges work well in contemporary applications, while decorative edges add style to traditional décor. Rounded or curved edges are more forgiving than square ones if you bump into them. An edge typically overhangs the top of the work surface by 1 inch, but some materials look better with a deeper overhang. Just make sure it doesn't obstruct base drawers or doors.

△ Consider clipping or rounding countertop corners for safety.

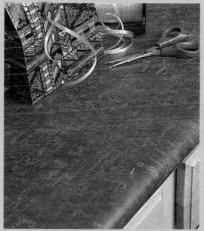

Ceramic Tile

Made from pressed clay and sealed with a glaze. Available in solid or mottled colors as well as textured or embossed surfaces. Durable. Stands up to hot pots, moisture, and dings. Can chip and crack, but individual tiles can be replaced. Regular grout needs to be sealed; newer epoxy-based grout deters staining and bacteria. Innovative sink options, including a sink made of tiles, are available. Use anywhere a flat surface is not required. $–$$

Laminate

Made up of layers of protective finish, printed design, and composite backing bonded together. Wide choice of colors, patterns, and visual or real textures, such as honed stone or metal. Limited edging options. Visible seams. Less durable than other materials. Stain resistant and easy to clean but will scratch and burn; protection such as cutting boards required. Use with above-mounted sink. Does not require professional installation. $

△ A design cut into a double ogee edge works well with paneled doors in a traditional kitchen.

BEFORE A 40-year-old kitchenette in a converted downtown commercial space was hardly this couple's dream kitchen. Its turquoise appliances and old wood cabinets provided little function and no architectural interest. But the new owners saw potential in the open studio setup. With some careful planning and a mix of luxurious materials, they created the social venue they had always envisioned.

AFTER To maintain the airy feel of the space, a large corner plan opens to other living areas, with a generous island for food preparation and casual dining. The high-grade stainless-steel appliances give the space a contemporary, industrial character, warmed by cherry and birch cabinetry and two colors of ultra-durable quartz countertops. In order to handle these larger-budget items, the owners chose a less expensive vinyl floor that looks like natural stone but is more resilient and easier to clean and maintain. For another view, see pages 10–11.

◄ **VERSATILITY AND CONVENIENCE** A built-in oven has both microwave and convection modes. The cabinetry beneath it features a pullout cutting board and two shallow drawers to keep cooking utensils and potholders on hand.

BEFORE The once popular practice of using ceiling-mounted cabinetry to divide a space was what these homeowners liked least about their old kitchen. The room was big enough, but the cabinets interrupted its flow. They wanted to open up the space and provide room for a casual eating area.

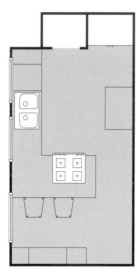

AFTER Existing Mexican tile flooring inspired the room's color palette and played a leading role in directing the homeowners' remodeling decisions. Once the ceiling-mounted cabinets were removed and the space was opened up, the finishes were key to brightening the space. Now, warm, mocha-glazed cabinets, olive sponge-painted walls, and deep terra-cotta accent tiles give the room its contemporary style. A freestanding island and a wider peninsula make the room comfortable for entertaining. Moving the water heater from a closet in the kitchen to a place below the house created room for the walk-in pantry.

what a great idea

finish with paint

A cream base coat, olive paint, and copper glaze make up the soft faux finish on the kitchen walls. To create this treatment, first apply a base coat of the cream-colored paint. While it dries, fill each of three plastic squirt bottles with one kind of paint: the base color, the olive, and the copper glaze. When the base coat has dried, follow the steps at right to sponge-paint the wall.

STEP 1: Holding the sponge in one hand, drizzle the olive paint horizontally across it. Then spread the base color vertically across the sponge. Sparingly add the copper glaze in a circular motion over the sponge.

▲ With a combination of wall cabinets, base cabinets, and an open-shelf bookcase, the homeowners created a built-in storage unit for the back wall. The backsplash, composed of tumbled marble and patterned tile, pulls together the colors of the floor, cabinets, and solid-surface countertop.

When the sponge is dry, repeat steps 1 and 2, applying only one set of the three colors to keep you from getting too much paint on the sponge. Continue sponging until the wall is completely covered, applying more paint to the sponge when necessary.

STEP 2: Using both hands, fold the sponge so the sides meet, lightly mixing colors.

STEP 3: Repeat steps 1 and 2 on top of the paint already blended on the sponge.

STEP 4: Using a light touch, apply the paint to the wall.

Lowe's Shopping List

Materials and Tools

- American Tradition, Vanilla Steam #2006-10C, semi-gloss
- American Tradition, Filoli Yew #5008-2B, semi-gloss
- Valspar Decorative Effects copper glaze
- measuring buckets
- natural sponge
- 3 empty plastic squirt bottles

Skill level: Beginner

Rough cost estimate: $75*

Rough time estimate: 1 day

*Does not include applicable taxes, which vary by market, or the cost of tools.

SPONGING TECHNIQUE

Work in one small area at a time. Lightly and randomly dab the sponge on the wall to avoid a contrived look. Hold the sponge at the same angle each time you touch the wall.

SOME OLDER KITCHENS may have everything—appliances, cabinets, and walls—in the right place but not in the desired style. In such kitchens, new materials and appliances can transform the space. Seven makeovers on the following pages provide idea-rich examples of how to restyle a kitchen.

BEFORE In this kitchen, the old floor plan was the only thing worth keeping. The work triangle—with the sink, cooktop, and refrigerator on three adjacent walls—provided an efficient workspace away from the traffic flow. But the cabinet doors were dated and hanging crookedly. The appliances were old, the wallpaper was discolored, the lighting was horrible, and the gold vinyl floor had to go.

AFTER The homeowners knew they wanted to splurge on good cabinetry, so they chose mocha-glazed maple to add warmth to the room. Removing the soffits above the old cabinets brought a sophisticated, seamless look to the kitchen and made room for 42-inch wall cabinets, increasing storage volume. Crown moulding finished the joint between the cabinetry and the ceiling.

▶ **TRADE-OFF** Energy-efficient appliances were also on the wish list. To offset the initial cost, the homeowners selected a less expensive plastic laminate countertop. Its concrete look complements the cabinetry and the new tile floor in both tone and texture.

▲ LAYERED LIGHTING The old ceiling fixture made way for seven recessed cans placed strategically around the room for general and task functions (see pages 52–53). Under-cabinet lighting illuminates the countertop workspaces.

LOWE'S INSTALLATION SERVICES
Remember that Lowe's provides professional installation services for many products, including flooring, appliances, cabinets, countertops, and ceiling lights and fans. Lowe's uses only licensed and insured installers. For more information, ask your local Lowe's.

BEFORE A 1970s kitchen remodel disregarded this home's English cottage style. Broken appliances and a rotten countertop created a room that was not only unattractive but dysfunctional. In undertaking their makeover, the new homeowners wanted to integrate the kitchen with the home's architecture.

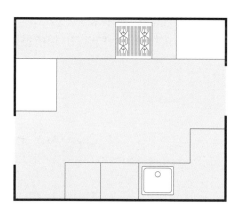

AFTER Color played a big part in the design solution for this new European farm-style kitchen. Mustard walls, green cabinets, gold counters, and a red floor create a cozy and welcoming ambience in a relatively small space.

By using open shelves on the upper walls and at the end of base cabinets, the homeowners reinforced the style and made room to exhibit their collection of ceramic pottery. Open shelving also saved money and allowed them to splurge on stainless-steel appliances that coordinate with the style and color of the kitchen. The homeowners bought shelves and brackets and painted them.

▲ OVEN CENTRAL A wall oven and microwave are close to the cooktop but out of the way of family traffic. The stainless-steel finish matches the cabinet hardware and kitchen accessories.

◄ HOOD HIGHLIGHT
A custom-made vent hood, painted the same color as the cabinetry, serves as the kitchen's focal point. A stainless bar below it can hold pots or utensils.

► VINTAGE LOOK No farmhouse kitchen is complete without a white porcelain sink. This wall-mounted model has an antique-style faucet and is deep enough to wash a big pot or bathe a baby.

Kitchen continues ▶

▶ Kitchen continued

◀ LIGHTING STYLE
Pendant lamps hanging between the kitchen and eating area add old-fashioned charm.

▼ KITCHEN SCENE Cutting a hole in the wall between the kitchen and breakfast nook was a lot less expensive than tearing down the whole wall. The pass-through and counter allow family members or guests to visit with the cooks. They also open up the windowless kitchen to outside light.

SAFETY TIPS

It's important to make safety a priority in your home. Always keep a **fire extinguisher** where you can reach it quickly and easily, and be sure it's appropriate to the location. The extinguisher shown here provides protection for kitchens, vehicles, and marine applications. The instructions are simple and visual, and the safety pin is easy to pull. Extinguishers with brushed finishes, such as this one, match stainless-steel appliances.

Install **smoke detectors** as required by local codes. When buying an alarm, look for the kind with a hush button to silence it quickly in non-dangerous situations.

A **carbon monoxide monitor** detects this toxic gas in your home. A digital display shows current levels and recent peaks. A loud alarm signals dangerously high levels.

the kitchen work triangle

FOR AN EFFICIENT KITCHEN PLAN, the three most heavily used work areas—the refrigerator, sink, and cooktop—should be placed so that the lines between them form a triangle in which no single leg is shorter than 4 feet or longer than 9 feet. The most efficient work triangles are found in galley, U-shaped, and L-shaped kitchen designs. If the distance between opposite walls is wide enough, you can build an island in the center of the room and install a cooktop or sink there.

GALLEY STYLE A galley layout consists of two parallel walls, with entry and exit at each end. This narrow layout makes the best use of a small space, especially when one major appliance can be placed on the second wall. Locating the refrigerator and microwave near one end minimizes traffic flow through the work space. Put upper cabinets on both walls to maximize storage.

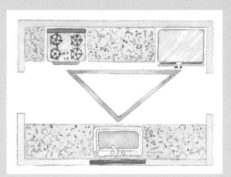

U-SHAPED When you have enough distance between opposite walls, use a U-shaped arrangement to provide maximum cabinet storage and counter space. This is considered by many to be the most efficient kitchen layout possible. Use a lazy Susan in the corner base cabinets to maximize storage. If possible, include a large window and/or skylights to keep the space light.

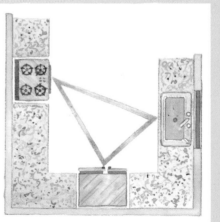

L-SHAPED This layout provides plenty of counter workspace and room for two cooks. The work triangle is efficient, with minimum traffic interruption. Another advantage is that it can accommodate an island if the area is spacious enough. The corner is prominent. If you don't put the sink there, consider storage options such as cabinets, open shelving, or an appliance garage to avoid dead space.

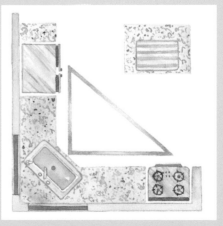

BEFORE While still serviceable, the old black-and-white kitchen felt cold and in need of a face-lift. By leaving all the appliances' locations intact, the homeowners were able to replace the cabinets, appliances, and surfaces without any major plumbing or mechanical work.

AFTER Natural colors and materials keep the kitchen light and soften its style. The homeowners started with the cabinetry, selecting wood-paneled doors with an almond glaze that accentuates the routed lines. Complementing the glaze, the midtone of the durable Corian countertops blends with the terra-cotta floor tiles. The size of the floor tiles (18 inches) makes the room appear more spacious, and the tone and texture mask dirt. Wall cabinets that run to the ceiling increase storage capacity significantly.

◄ Large drawers hold a lot but can become jumbled. Expandable organizers house utensils and control clutter.

▲ **DESK SET** One benefit of remodeling the kitchen was finding space for a new home-office workstation. It's a great place for kids to do homework while Mom or Dad cooks nearby. A tailor-made wall storage shelf keeps essentials from cluttering the desk surface.

◀ A country-style faucet goes well with the cabinetry hardware. Moulding around a new casement window echoes other wood trim in the room.

BEFORE A low ceiling and soffit made this small kitchen feel cramped and dated. Stark colors, closed cabinets, and poor lighting added to the gloomy and claustrophobic atmosphere.

AFTER Color pulls it together. A warm and simple color palette makes the room more inviting and integrates it with the contemporary style of the home. Different tones of red, with highlights of black and silver, unify the space. Note, for instance, how the red of the cherry base cabinetry is picked up in the red-gray slate tiles used on the backsplash, wall, and floor. The stainless-steel countertops, appliances, and hardware reflect light and add sparkle to the room, while the black vertical lines of the upper cabinets emphasize the room's newfound height—the homeowners removed the original flat ceiling and borrowed several feet from the attic.

▲ At one end of the kitchen, an efficient built-in desk and message center is tucked under a slender, double-sided glass cabinet suspended across an opening to the adjacent living room. The black granite serving counter to the left of the desk serves as an elegant transition between the rooms.

AFTER The homeowner concentrated on stylishly expanding storage capacity without blocking natural light. The most obvious solution was to remove the low soffit around the perimeter of the ceiling and install taller cabinets. The new cabinetry includes a special pedimented, ribbed-glass space set in front of the existing window. It acts as a screen, letting in daylight while blocking views of a neighboring house. Built-in halogen downlights make the glass-shelved interior glow softly at night. A strip of lighting under the adjacent cabinets illuminates a shallow shelf that can display crafts or hold frequently used condiments and spices.

BEFORE This kitchen lacked both style and storage, and the new owner, a furniture designer, wanted a look that reflected his attention to detail. The challenge was how to make the space look more contemporary and function more efficiently without enlarging it.

PULLOUTS The homeowner also made clever use of the notoriously inconvenient space above the refrigerator. The narrow cabinet to the left of the fridge is a side-facing pullout for spices, oils, and other cooking ingredients. Above the refrigerator are similar pullout units. A simple white tile countertop blends in with the walls.

storage

KEY TO A TIDY KITCHEN, and usually crucial to efficiency as well, storage can be the difference between an OK makeover and a wildly successful one. At Lowe's, you can review the options available from cabinet manufacturers as well as clever off-the-rack items.

Behind Doors What lurks behind closed doors can be chaos. Opt for organization with base-cabinet inserts like these.

▲ Pullout drawers allow for easy reach and a full view of what's stored inside a pantry.

▲ Efficient lazy Susan shelving keeps you from losing items in the dark recesses of your corner cabinets.

▲ Shallow rollout shelves are ideal for table linens.

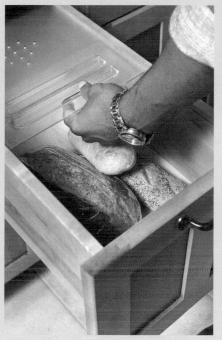

▲ A cork-lined drawer with slots helps organize knives and keeps blades sharper longer. Below, dividers separate flatware and serving utensils.

▲ A sliding acrylic lid turns a deep under counter drawer into a built-in breadbox. The ventilated lid keeps bread fresh. Place the drawer near the toaster for convenience.

▲ Just below waist height, deep drawers with removable dividers let you store and access heavy pots and pans—and their lids—without bending over. Build them close to the cooktop.

In Drawers
Shallow drawers are good for flatware and linens, while deeper styles can house cookware, dishes, and dry goods. Dividers and other add-ons customize the drawer for the items stored.

Hidden Storage
Look for unused space for small items you want to access quickly.

◄ Keep sponges and scrubbers out of sight in a tilt-down sink front. An organizer that attaches to the inside of a cupboard door stores larger cleaning items below.

BEFORE The homeowners liked the black-and-white motif of their kitchen, but it had inadequate storage and counter space and was ready for a makeover. When base-cabinet doors fell off and couldn't be replaced, the owners decided it was time to bring their old kitchen into the new century.

AFTER As avid cooks with young daughters, the homeowners had two goals: a room that would function well as a kitchen, plus a desk and a comfortable area for kids and guests. Their biggest challenge was to create more space within the existing walls. Their solution: Remove a peninsula counter that jutted out from one wall, needlessly dividing the room. They increased storage by adding ceiling-height cabinets around what was once a freestanding refrigerator.

◄ **COUNTRY COLOR** Design decisions were driven by the homeowners' desire for a country-style kitchen, which translated into white beadboard cupboards and ceiling, a backsplash of white tile, and a durable pine-like laminate floor. The multi-color palette comes from a favorite painting. If you use such a complex combination of colors, it is best to make one color dominant. In this kitchen, the red walls add the punch that was missing in the old white room.

▲ Across from the window seat, a solid-surface countertop does double duty as home office and kid space.

► A slender pullout base cabinet makes clever use of a narrow space. It also stores spices and sauces near the stove.

BEFORE This galley-style kitchen lacked character and any connection with the patio garden just outside. Wall cupboards on opposite walls created a narrow corridor that felt oppressive.

AFTER The sophisticated new design is sleek and efficient. Running cabinets on only one wall keeps the kitchen open. The clean lines of the cabinets and counters contribute to the sense of spaciousness, as does the lack of clutter: Cabinets, drawers, cubbies, and hooks provide dedicated places for kitchenware, cookbooks, and dry goods. The most innovative change was the addition of a Dutch door at the end of the room. The top acts as a pass-through window for outdoor dining, while the homeowners unload groceries through the bottom. A counter running in front of it makes an open-air spot for informal meals.

▼ COOL PALETTE

It's the color scheme that brings the room together. Moss-green cabinetry, slate-blue countertops and windows, and natural wood trim echo the garden just beyond the Dutch door. The cool colors create a serene and tranquil effect that enhances the feeling of openness.

▲ CREATIVE CLOSURE

Hanging the door on a barn-door track outside the kitchen keeps the look streamlined and open.

◄ BUILT-IN STORAGE

A cabinet customized for a narrow wall at one end of the kitchen includes both closed compartments and cubbies sized to fit items such as wine bottles and a stack of mixing bowls. Deep drawers hold large stockpots out of sight, and hooks hang the cooks' favorite pans.

IF YOUR KITCHEN IS
functional but lacks visual pizzazz, conserve money by playing up the assets you have. As the kitchen makeovers on the next few pages prove, you can develop an exciting new look with a can of paint as well as new hardware, fixtures, and countertops. These transformations offer creative ways to get the biggest bang for your buck.

BEFORE Though in relatively good shape, this kitchen was terribly outdated, sporting unappealing floral wallpaper along with tired and stained white vinyl flooring. The once bright white cabinets had become dingy, faded, and worn. Not having an abundance of time or money to put toward a major remodel, the homeowners opted for a savvy, strategic redo of the kitchen.

AFTER Countertops take center stage here. The texture and warm gold tones of the granite make the biggest statement in this inviting new space, and they provide the color cue for the rest of the room. Hanging cabinets were removed to open up the kitchen to the breakfast area. The remaining cabinets, which provided ample storage, were given new life with a coat of warm yellow paint that is the perfect complement to the new countertops. Twelve-inch-square ceramic floor tiles also blend well with the color scheme. As final touches, new hardware, a metal chandelier, and colorful window treatments enhance the kitchen's traditional style.

▶ **DUAL-PURPOSE DESK** A great bonus in a kitchen is a spot to pay bills and compose grocery lists. These homeowners were able to lower a section of countertop to make room for a desk. Out of the way of the main kitchen traffic, it can double as a serving area.

◀ **SLEEK SINK** An undermounted stainless-steel sink and a pull-out faucet with sprayer maintain the sleek look of the countertops. The sink's seamless design also makes cleanup and maintenance easier, as there is no lip to catch debris.

BEFORE Dark wood can make a small kitchen feel even smaller, as the cabinets in this old kitchen make clear. The homeowners, a young couple on a tight budget, felt that the only way they could afford to replace the 1960s appliances and update the countertops and the floor was to leave the old cabinets in place.

AFTER Reface, don't replace. That was the solution here. Fortunately, the original routed cabinet doors were not in bad shape. They just needed a bit of an update, so the homeowners used embossed wood trim to disguise the routed grooves. A coat of soft taupe semigloss paint on the cabinets and walls transformed the space. A tile backsplash, set in a diamond pattern that mimics the new tile floor, gives additional character to the room.

To provide a touch of contrast to the light colors, a delicate embossed wood appliqué adorns the cornice above the sink.

antiquing wood appliqués

Wooden appliqués come in a large assortment of designs and sizes, and more can be special-ordered. To replicate the aged look of the trim piece shown here and to apply it to a wall, cabinet, or other piece of furniture, follow these steps:

STEP 1: Paint the appliqué with American Accents Colonial Red. Before the paint dries, wipe it down with a rag, allowing the wood to show through. This will give it a worn appearance.

STEP 2: After the paint dries, apply a thin coat of mocha glaze. This will contribute to the aged appearance.

STEP 3: After the glaze has dried completely, apply wood glue to the back of the appliqué (following the glue manufacturer's instructions) and press it into place. Hold it until it sets.

Lowe's Shopping List

Millwork
• carving

Paint and Materials
• American Tradition, Cliveden Henna Red #1008-7A, semi-gloss
• glaze (American Tradition, Mocha #94825)
• wood glue (#86091)
• paintbrushes
• rag

Skill level: Beginner
Rough cost estimate: $40*
Rough time estimate: ½ day

*Does not include applicable taxes, which vary by market, or the cost of tools.

family
spaces

THE SHARED AREAS OF YOUR HOME express the personalities of your family. Making over the entry, eating areas, living spaces, and home office can help you customize each room so that it beckons both family members and friends to come in, enjoy, and relax.

The remodeling strategies in this chapter will help you bring out the potential in your home's common spaces. The secret can be as simple as adding character with new color, lighting, and accessories. You might turn a maze of impractical small spaces into one functional room or convert an unused bedroom into a home office. You'll find lots of examples here of how to carry out anything from small changes to a dramatic transformation.

Start the process with a family conversation so each member can share ideas. Family spaces are for all of you to enjoy.

This spare room in a basement had little appeal for adults, let alone children. The kid-friendly makeover brought in primary colors, pint-size furniture, a comfortable rug, and a crafts area. See pages 58–59 for more details.

THE ENTRYWAY SETS THE STYLE and tone of your home and leaves an important first impression. Inside, a hallway provides a transition from one area to the next and can become an attraction all its own. On these pages, see how fresh looks were created in relatively inexpensive ways.

BEFORE White walls, dark flooring, and a stained wooden door created a harsh contrast to the softer tones in the rest of the house. A single ceiling fixture cast dim light on this uninviting entry.

AFTER The transformation began with a neutral color palette for the door and walls. The textured wallpaper in a warm beige blends the entry visually with adjacent rooms, amplifying the sense that this is a rich, integral part of the house. A hardwood floor adds a burnished glow to the space, and a paneled wooden door and carved moulding reinforce the home's classic style. The gold finish of the framed mirror and wall fixtures lends elegance to the entry, also shown on on page 7.

▼ **BRIGHT AND SECURE** The home needed a new storm door to protect the main one and to provide extra security. The glass door allows light to flow into the house when the wooden door is open; it has a multi-point locking system.

three looks for one hall

In a hallway, different wall treatments, flooring, lighting, accessories, and door hardware create distinct and striking style in an unexpected place.

CASUAL If a hallway is adjacent to a back or side door, it can double as a mudroom. Wall panels, shown here in warm yellow and available in an array of other colors and textures, dramatically brighten up this back hallway. Mini pendants of red glass and an area rug made of striped carpet add splashes of color and personality. With robe hooks on the wall, a sturdy bench below, and a set of storage baskets, you have everything you need.

TRADITIONAL Deep red wallpaper provides a mix of color and pattern, complemented by the dark, rich finish on the hardwood floor. The traditional theme is accentuated by decorative details such as the rustic bronze hall table and lamp. A unique door of etched glass provides a focal point, while the red and gold of the rug tie the color scheme together.

CONTEMPORARY To create a modern look, start with a simple color palette. In this hallway, a single color is used on the wall and trim, with the door a darker shade of the same gray. White wall sconces and a doorknob with a satin nickel finish add visual interest within the same color mood. This scheme provides a neutral canvas for contemporary art and a color-block carpet in bold geometric designs. You can arrange the carpet blocks in an afternoon, installing them with peel-and-stick adhesive.

WHEREVER YOU GATHER TO EAT, be it a formal dining room, breakfast nook, or kitchen table, you want it to be a special place that inspires great meals and good conversation. Wall color, lighting, flooring, and ceiling and window treatments all play a part in setting the tone for this space.

BEFORE Dark wood and heavy cabinetry, along with old-fashioned lighting, contributed to the oppressive atmosphere of this space. The open floor plan had potential, though, so the homeowners decided to work with it to create a great place to gather.

AFTER This remodel was all about letting in light. At the rear, a glass-block window replaces part of the wall of cabinets, and a new skylight above the kitchen floods the room with daylight. Pendant cable lights above the serving counter suggest a boundary to the kitchen, while a modern chandelier helps delineate the dining area. In this open plan, the light tones of the maple-veneer cabinets become part of the dining area's color scheme, which continues with warm yellow walls. The area rug picks up the darker wood tones of the chair seatbacks and cabinetry trim, providing a good counterpoint to the light color scheme.

BEFORE A single dining-room window allowed a view but no access to a spacious deck behind the house. The homeowners wanted to add doors, but the window opening was higher than the top of a normal door.

AFTER A pair of French doors replaced the window, with a custom transom to fill in the extra height of the old window opening. Now light pours inside and diners enjoy the lovely view of the deck and garden beyond. The doors also enhance indoor-outdoor entertaining.

French doors open the dining room to the deck.

BEFORE Wallpaper with a large floral print once may have been high style for a dining area, but when a young family bought this older home, they knew it had to go. The white vinyl flooring was also begging to be removed.

AFTER Nature dominates. From the warm tones of the granite counter-top and the sunny yellow walls to the antique pine table and the rattan chairs, every surface in the room evokes colors and textures of nature. The homeowners wanted an attractive dining area that would complement the adjoining kitchen (see pages 40–41) and achieved it by keeping the color palette consistent. The warm reds and golds of the valance add energy. Finishing touches, such as an iron chandelier and a live fern, give the room additional character.

FABRIC POINTERS

Fabrics radiate personality with their colors, patterns, and textures and can set the mood of a room. Follow these tips when using them in any décor:

- With large quantities of fabric in small spaces, select prints on a light-colored background for a soft, airy feel.
- Geometrics—checks, plaids, and stripes—coordinate nicely with other patterns when the principal colors are the same. Mix and match until you find the right set, and don't ignore the ready-made combinations that are offered by many manufacturers.
- When using several different fabrics, vary the pattern scale. For instance, a small floral design might be combined with large-scale plaids and stripes.
- Check wallpaper books for coordinating fabrics that can be special-ordered. Allow time for delivery if you purchase materials this way.

layered lighting

AN IMPORTANT ELEMENT in home décor, lighting not only illuminates work areas and highlights our surroundings but also enables us to perceive color and texture. In designing a lighting scheme for each room, first determine what kind of light you need—general, task, or accent—and where you need it. The most effective lighting schemes use a combination of types to create a layered effect. There are several kinds of fixtures. While some provide only one kind of light, others produce all three.

SPOTLIGHT ON LIGHTING

- In general, to create an inviting atmosphere, use three to five light sources in a room.
- In most rooms, aim to provide varying intensities of light. Add dimmer switches or use three-way bulbs for flexibility. For example, when the kids do homework at the dinner table, you'll need strong task lighting. But when guests arrive for a dinner party, you'll want ambient lighting on a dimmer, with accent lights on the walls.
- To make rooms interesting, vary the height of the light sources. The differing heights add depth by creating separate areas of light and shade.
- Lighting collections have a full range of fixture types in one finish and style. Fixtures from the same collection within a room create a unified look.
- Remember, because dark colors absorb light, you'll need to use more lighting in rooms decorated in dark colors than in rooms with light colors.

General

General, or ambient, lighting can provide overall illumination in any room, large or small. Almost any kind of overhead system provides good ambient lighting. Recessed cans, chandeliers, and ceiling fixtures are great options. Some floor lamps, including torchères, which bounce light onto the ceiling, also do the trick nicely.

FLOOR LAMP

Task

In spaces for specific activities, such as brushing your teeth, showering, cooking, reading, or sewing, you want to light the space without intruding upon it. Control the intensity with the wattage of the bulb and with the bulb's distance from the work area. Consider recessed, cable, and pendant lighting as well as desk, table, or floor lamps when you need to light a defined area.

CABLE LIGHTING

Accent

When you want to illuminate a specific object, to emphasize different textures and surfaces in a room, or just to add a decorative element, use accent lighting. Track lights and recessed canisters with pinhole or eyeball fixtures are perfect for lighting artwork. Sconces throw a wash of light along a wall. Add dimmers for altering the mood.

RECESSED EYEBALL LIGHT

Vary your choices to give your room several kinds of illumination.

DOWNLIGHT

CHANDELIER

DESK LAMP

PENDANT LIGHT

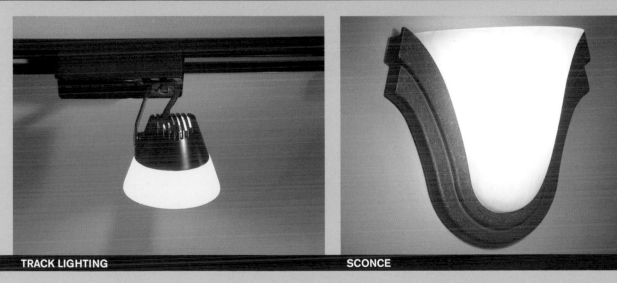
TRACK LIGHTING

SCONCE

THESE ROOMS ARE GATHERING SPOTS,

casual places where family and friends can chat, play games, celebrate, watch movies, or just relax. In a home that doesn't have a family room, a makeover can transform an underutilized space, such as a garage, basement, or porch, into a room you all use and love.

BEFORE The owners of this home noticed that whenever they had a party, everyone ended up in the garage, which was on the way to the backyard. So they turned the garage into a comfortable and casual place for family members and friends to relax together.

AFTER Since the garage was adjacent to the kitchen and breakfast area, they were able to knock out a wall and create one big great room. A stained wooden ceiling and hardwood floors now tie the old and new spaces together. New windows and French doors bring light into the space by day, while track lights along the beams provide good illumination at night. A close match for the kitchen cabinets, the family-room storage holds games, books, and electronic equipment.

GARAGE CONVERSION TIPS

- If your garage has underutilized space, use interior walls or partitions to redefine it. Consider framing in a corner closet, bathroom, laundry room, home office, or mudroom.
- Visually link adjacent spaces by repeating a color palette or patterns. Cover the original garage slab with the same flooring or rugs as you've used in the adjoining room, or add framing to bring the garage floor level with that of the adjacent space.
- Add skylights, windows, or French doors to brighten the new room.
- Insulate the outside walls and roof to increase energy efficiency.
- If it's too expensive or labor-intensive to extend existing heating ducts into the remodeled space, add a gas fireplace that's rated as a room heater or install a clean-burning EPA-certified woodstove.

BEFORE This growing family needed more space, and the old kitchen was the place to look for it. With only enough room for a breakfast table, the kitchen was cramped, plus the stained wooden paneling and brick fireplace wall made it dark and gloomy.

AFTER Cheerful terra-cotta and peachy yellow paint pull two spaces together, creating one beautiful great room. Formed when the homeowners broke through a brick wall to expand into the garage, the new family room is light and airy thanks to the bright color scheme and new windows on facing walls. Thoughtfully placed recessed lighting accents the room at night. On each side of the stairs, waist-high base cabinets add storage, as do the bookshelves and an entertainment cabinet flanking a new gas fireplace centered on the rear wall.

AFTER The new den is barely recognizable as the same space. With hard work and a good sense of design, the homeowners turned challenges into advantages. They had to remake the staircase, and in the process they discovered they could convert a closet under the stairwell into a small refreshment area. Since all wiring needed to be rerouted, they wired for a surround-sound system. And with the addition of lumber and moulding, the unsightly support posts became architectural columns that give character to the new 500-square-foot room.

BEFORE A dark unfinished basement that contained two primary rooms, a laundry room, an unfinished bath, and a storage area was the best spot in the house for a versatile family space. Fortunately, it had no moisture problems and there were two good-sized windows.

▶ **BEVERAGE STATION** A sink, a counter, and a compact refrigerator put cold drinks and snacks close at hand when the family is relaxing or entertaining.

MUSIC AREA The smaller of the two primary rooms became a large nook where the husband can practice drumming. Ductwork at the back of the area was covered with gypsum drywall and painted the same color as the walls to create the illusion of a higher ceiling.

COLUMN COVER-UP You can cleverly conceal a support post with a little lumber and decorative moulding. Start by determining the width of your finished columns, considering their proportion in relation to the room. Slender columns work best in smaller rooms with low ceilings, while wider ones are suitable for large spaces with high ceilings. This column is 8 inches square. The side panels, of medium-density fiberboard, are attached to 2 by 10 collar blocks at top and bottom (above right). The capital (the top) was created from three different moulding styles: a 3⅝″ crown, a 3¼″ base trim turned upside down, and a 1⅜″ rope strip.

For complete how-to instructions, go to Lowes.com/columncoverup.

DESIGN DETAILS The new room is now bright thanks to its color scheme and sunlight from the two windows. Flush-mounted blinds modulate the natural light. Beige berber carpeting covers the entire floor, while a colorful rug defines the sitting area. Louvered doors, cut in half and stained, create a bold backdrop for a collection of botanical prints, which hang from red grosgrain ribbon tied to antique brass knobs.

CHILDREN'S ROOMS

Kids need space to spread out, play games, do crafts, or entertain friends. When bedrooms aren't large enough to contain all this activity, or when you want the extra noise out of your hearing range, it's great to have a playroom or teen hangout.

BEFORE Sometimes it takes more than just an old sofa and carpet to attract kids to a play area. While this basement room offered a space away from Mom and Dad, the children rarely used it because it was so uninviting.

▲ **CRAFTY KIDS** Having a dedicated spot to do crafts keeps messy art materials off the rug and furniture. This space-efficient art station is composed of 12-by-36-inch shelves on support brackets. Cork tiles are attached to the wall with metal furniture glides.

▲ **HANG IT UP** Art supplies are within arm's reach thanks to a handy 38-drawer storage bin on the wall. Beneath the bin is a tube of builder's paper hung on a cut-down white wooden drapery rod with ball finials and matching supports.

AFTER Bright colors—yellow walls and a fire-engine-red entertainment center—give the remodeled playroom (also shown on pages 44–45) a cheerful, kid-friendly atmosphere. Laminate flooring that resembles slate with grout lines adds contemporary flair and has the added benefits of being resilient and easy to clean. The fun block-pattern rug in shades of red, off-white, and blue is made of cotton rugs whipstitched together with a large upholstery needle. An upholstery shop can do this for you if you prefer.

◄ **FACE-LIFT** The dark fireplace wall was transformed with two coats of textured-sand paint in a warm off-white. The parents encourage their budding artists by framing and prominently displaying their children's paintings, which also add character to the space.

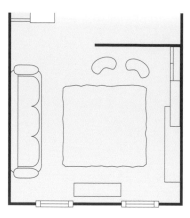

BEFORE The homeowners wanted a place for their teenage daughters to watch television, do homework, or entertain friends. An unfinished basement, already plumbed for a bath, seemed like the right spot, but ductwork, ventilation, and wiring systems posed challenges.

AFTER The new teen room offers space to relax as well as storage and display areas. Its main walls were kept white as a backdrop for the girls' growing collection of original art, which cued the colors of the accent walls and the special-order blinds. Created to camouflage ductwork, the lower display ledge adds architectural interest as well. Wood-laminate planks installed on a cushioned backing over the concrete subfloor create a surface that will not warp or be damaged by minor cracks or imperfections in the slab. A similar ceiling system visually opens up the space and accommodates varied lighting.

▶ **SODAS AND SNACKS** A refreshment center is a real convenience in any teen hangout. This one has a mini refrigerator for drinks and snacks as well as storage in off-the-rack wall and base cabinets. An easily installed white laminate countertop was cut to fit the space.

NEW ADDITION

Sometimes the only way to gain space is to go out of your home's footprint. In this case, the homeowners incorporated a teen haven in an addition they were building onto their house. This versatile space serves the kids now but will convert to a guest suite or home office once they've moved out.

The teenagers were given decorating control of their space, and they chose a cool palette of colors that would appeal to both boys and girls. On the floor, carpet tiles let the kids create their own playful arrangement in one afternoon. The parents insisted on plenty of storage to control clutter, so a simple wire shelving unit serves as an entertainment center. As a fun twist, the kids hung outdoor wall lanterns on either side of the doors, providing good ambient light.

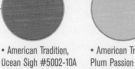

- American Tradition, Ocean Sigh #5002-10A
- American Tradition, Plum Passion #6007-5B
- American Tradition, Pontoon White #7006-13
- American Tradition, Sailboat #4005-5B

▲ ALL THE AMENITIES

Standard cabinetry and laminate countertops made it easy and affordable to set up a snack station. With both a mini refrigerator and a microwave, the kids can grab a soda and make popcorn without setting foot in the home's kitchen. Covering the windows and French doors, sage-green Roman shades moderate the natural light.

carpet tiles

For wall-to-wall carpeting or an area rug, a modular flooring system made of carpet tiles is both fun and affordable. Mix and match patterns, styles, and colors for a unique design, or use a single color for a seamless look.

- Peel-and-stick installation makes it easy to cover an entire room in just a few hours.
- Tiles can be pulled up one at a time for cleaning or replacement.
- Visit Lowes.com and search with the keyword "flooring" to find the latest products available at Lowe's.

what a great idea

WHETHER YOU RUN A BUSINESS out of your home or spend part of your day doing deskwork, it's great to have a quiet, organized space you can call your own. Sometimes the location for a home office is obvious, such as in a corner of your kitchen or in a spare bedroom. Other times it takes finding unused space in a basement or closet.

BEFORE This girl's bedroom got no use after she went off to college. The homeowners decided to convert this room into a home office, giving their daughter the guest room when she came home for visits. Located just off the foyer, the office needed to be as stylish as it was functional.

AFTER Warm earth tones, rich cabinetry, and soft yet useful illumination create a study in elegance. French doors bring in light but shut out noise. Additional task lighting is supplied by subtle under-cabinet fixtures above the desk area. Hardwood flooring replaced pale carpeting to give the room a more masculine look.

▶ ON DISPLAY Three floor-to-ceiling bookcases match the desk unit and, placed together on one wall, hold books and a camera collection. Adjustable shelves accommodate items of various heights.

◀ BONUS STORAGE With wire shelving, a former clothes closet stores office supplies. Gray cardboard containers and magazine butlers keep loose items organized.

▶ CLEVER CADDY The computer's CPU resides under the desk on a caddy made of plywood and casters. The wheels make it easy to move the CPU for cleaning and help keep the floor scratch-free. The caddy was stained in a mahogany finish to blend with the cabinetry and then sealed with polyurethane to protect the wood.

🖱 Log on to Lowes.com/computercaddy for detailed how-to building instructions.

BEFORE   A long, blank basement wall was the obvious place to locate a work and study area for these homeowners and their two preteen children. The challenge was maximizing the space to achieve lots of storage as well.

AFTER   Function and durability were the highest priorities in this makeover. The homeowners chose light earth tones to brighten the space and durable finishes that are easy to maintain. Selecting less expensive cabinetry without knobs meant they could afford to line the entire wall with upper and base cabinets. A long stretch of inexpensive laminate countertop in a rusty tone provides more than enough space for the computer and other office equipment. To warm up the room, the entire floor is covered in nylon carpet, which is both durable and resistant to dirt and mildew. A necessity, the drop-down ceiling proved to be an advantage when it came to lighting, as the panels made it a snap to add wiring and new recessed lights.

CREATING THE PERFECT HOME OFFICE

Answering some questions will help you design and arrange a home office that addresses your specific needs.

- How much time will you spend in the office?
- What type of work will you do? This will affect the amount of space and the type of work surfaces you'll need.
- Will the office center around the computer system? The countertops may need to have circles cut out for cables.
- How much privacy do you need?

▲ CUBBIES AND SHELVES There's plenty of space above the desk area to keep stationery, reference books, and bills within arm's reach. Other supplies can be organized in drawers and behind the closed doors.

◄ A PLACE FOR EVERYTHING Tall pantry cabinets at each end of the desk units store oversized supplies such as wrapping paper, paint cans, and tall vases and candlesticks.

DOUBLE DUTY Tucked away upstairs, an attic room makes an ideal spot for a quiet office or multipurpose family room. In this case, the home-owners wanted both. Mom wanted a place to manage her day-to-day household chores while the kids were at school, and the children needed somewhere to do homework, use the computer, entertain friends, and accommodate overnight guests. Now remodeled, the space does double duty with aplomb. Vivid red paint enlivens the room and emphasizes the walls' interesting angles. Light wood cabinetry and carpet, plus black accents, reinforce the contemporary style.

◄ MULTIPURPOSE NOOK An existing dormer window accommodates a window seat almost 7 feet long, constructed of shallow wall cabinetry (for more storage) and a countertop surface. When the cushion is removed, the seat makes a secondary work or play surface.

▲ STYLISH STORAGE Three black shelves provide storage and display areas. At right, an angled corner cabinet, painted the same red as the walls, hides an entertainment center.

◄ WELL-CONSIDERED ACCENTS The wood blinds match the cabinetry; their tape ties in with the black shelves and accessories.

► ON TRACK Three track lights can be angled to provide general or task lighting, supplementing the natural light that streams through the large double window.

BEFORE This home-owner needed her guest room to also serve as a hiding place for her computer and television station. She wanted an industrial look to complement the contemporary style of her condominium.

AFTER With the right materials, the bedroom closet provided a creative solution. Stock materials and accessories create a compact work area that functions superbly and looks crisp.

CLEVER SOLUTIONS

Shelving tracks run the entire height of the back wall, and 10- and 12-inch-deep shelves at various levels accommodate different sizes of equipment. The lowest shelf, with an additional wall attachment to support heavy items, serves as a desk.

In keeping with the industrial theme is a metal tool chest, just the right size to support the television and to store videos and office supplies. The homeowner's most creative idea was to cover the wall behind the desk with metal sheeting to form a large magnetic bulletin board.

Track lights hidden behind the doorstop shine directly on the shelves. As a final touch, frosted glass doors obscure the closet's contents and add contemporary elegance to the room.

Found space: behind closed doors is a well–outfitted entertainment nook with an efficient workstation.

wall-mounted cabinet

WHEN A DESK SURFACE is not big enough to support a hutch, a wall-mounted cabinet provides storage and display space. Follow the steps below to make your own.

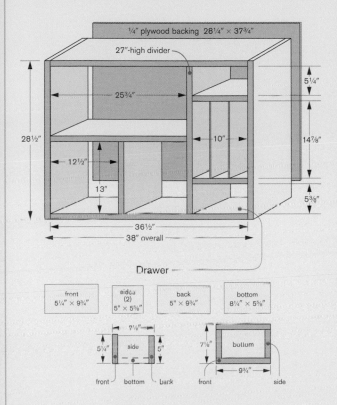

¼" plywood backing 28¼" × 37¾"
27"-high divider
25¾"
28½"
12½"
13"
36½"
38" overall
5¼"
14⅞"
10"
5⅜"

Drawer

front
5¼" × 9¾"

sides
(2)
5" × 5⅝"

back
5" × 9¾"

bottom
8¼" × 5⅝"

7¼"
5¼"   side   5"
front   bottom   back

7⅛"   bottom
9¾"
front   side

STEP 1: Cut out all the pieces on the cut list. Be sure to cut the backing square to ensure that the entire unit stays square. Sand edges and rough spots. Lay out the boards, marking with a ruler and pencil where they intersect.

STEP 2: In the two 10 × 8-inch boards, cut equidistant ¼- by ⅜-inch-deep matching grooves for the plywood dividers.

STEP 3: Assemble the cabinet with a hammer and the finishing nails, working from the outside in and accurately lining up each board. Glue and nail on the backing using the wire brads. Assemble the drawer according to the diagram.

STEP 4: Measure and miter the moulding trim pieces; affix to the top and bottom of the cabinet with the finishing nails.

STEP 5: Countersink nails with a nailset; fill holes and sand. Caulk where necessary and prepare for painting.

STEP 6: Paint the cabinet with a finish that matches the trim in the room.

STEP 7: With the wood screws, hang the cabinet on the wall, making sure to attach it to wall studs.

CUT LIST

Use 1 × 8 pine for all parts except back and 15⅝" dividers, which are ¼-inch plywood

Part	Quantity	Length
top and bottom	2	36½ × 8"
sides	2	28½ × 8"
divider	1	13 × 8"
divider	1	27 × 8"
divider	1	25¾ × 8"
dividers	2	10 × 7¼"
back	1	28¼ × 37¾"
dividers	2	15⅝ × 8"
drawer front	1	5¼ × 9¾"
drawer sides	2	5 × 5⅝"
drawer back	1	5 × 9¾"
drawer bottom	1	8¼ × 5⅝"

Lowe's Shopping List

Millwork and Lumber*

- 5 (3-foot-long) 1 × 8 boards
- 2 (4-foot-long) 1 × 8 boards
- ½ panel (4 feet × 4 feet) ¼-inch plywood
- 1 (8-foot-long) piece of 2¾-inch crown moulding
- 1 (8-foot-long) piece of base trim of choice (approx. 2⅜ inches wide)

Materials and Hardware

- 1 box of (#17 × 1-inch) wire brads
- 1 box of (1½-inch) 4d finishing nails
- 1 package of (1½-inch) wood screws

Tools

- table saw
- tape measure
- hammer
- wood glue
- miter saw
- nailset
- sandpaper
- wood filler
- caulk and caulk gun
- paint

Skill level: Intermediate

Rough cost estimate: $60**

Rough time estimate: 2 days

*Availability varies by market.
**Does not include applicable taxes, which vary by market, or the cost of tools.

bedrooms

BEDROOMS ARE THE MOST PERSONAL LIVING SPACES IN THE HOUSE, reflecting the styles and preferences of the adults and children who occupy them. A great bedroom provides a welcome and safe retreat from the demands of everyday life as well as a place to sleep, dress, read, play, and sometimes work.

An adult or teen bedroom may include a reading chair, work desk, entertainment center, and even exercise equipment in addition to a bed and bureau. The ideal child's room has dedicated play and work areas as well as a clever storage system for toys. Along with appropriate lighting and easy-on-bare-feet flooring, these elements add up to a room that says "mine."

Any bedroom makeover should create a place its occupant loves and is happy in. To that end, take time for plenty of consultation and discussion. Even young children have strong opinions about their own spaces.

In this chapter, you'll see refurbished and remodeled bedrooms for both adults and kids, each of them a personal and pleasing space.

A good layout wasn't enough to make this a satisfactory master bedroom. Adding built-ins turned it into a true haven. For details, see page 76.

A SOOTHING AND SERENE master bedroom makes you feel good about getting up in the morning and welcomes you back after a hard day's work. To create this sanctuary, use a palette based on colors you love, add textures and patterns that express your style, and choose the most comfortable furniture you can find. You may be able to refresh and reuse what you have.

BEFORE This bedroom had a patched-together look, and no wonder. Everything but the bed was from the wife's childhood or college days. Now she and her husband, parents of a toddler and a newborn, wanted to create a retreat that would offer them comfort and grown-up style.

AFTER A set of throw pillows in a vibrant botanical pattern on a black background determined the room's color palette, starting with the subtle olive green on the walls. Rich red bedding and black accents balance the cool green. The ceiling is painted two shades lighter than the walls to add a sense of height to the room, and matching paint on the blades of the new ceiling fan helps the fixture blend in. In front of the window, a hand-me-down chair, re-covered in green linen to match the walls, provides a comfortable place to read. Orange piping adds pop.

STYLE ON A BUDGET

Don't let limited finances cramp your decorating style. Here are a few cost-effective ways you can give your home personality without going into debt.

- Add character to a blank wall with a stylish faux paint treatment. Paint creates the most impact for the least amount of money.
- Frame inexpensive posters from festivals or art exhibits. If you can't find a frame to fit the poster, try adding a mat cut to fit. Other great inexpensive wall decorations include children's artwork and collections such as old plates.
- Top an outdated nightstand with a round of plywood and a fabric skirt.
- Add casters to an old dresser drawer, then roll it under the bed for instant storage.

▲ **BUILT-IN LOOK** To stay within a tight budget, the homeowners installed unfinished bookshelves and painted them the same color as the walls, creating the look of built-ins without the cost. Each slender unit has three open shelves for display and a closed section below for storage.

▶ **INGENIOUS SOLUTION**
The two nightstands add clever and inexpensive storage as well. They are actually metal trash cans topped with 30-inch wood rounds. The cans hold items such as sweaters that aren't needed year-round.

one bedroom, three ways

Find your own style.

THIS TYPICAL BEDROOM in three styles shows how you can change the way a room looks and feels. Wall color, window treatment, lighting, and furniture are all elements in establishing a style and making a makeover work.

▲ DRAMATICALLY CONTEMPORARY

The elements of contemporary design include bold color palettes; clean, seamless lines; and modular storage solutions. In this room, the red-tone wraparound headboard contrasts dramatically with the light linen-colored walls. Bamboo blinds contribute a linear pattern over the window, while dark colors emphasize the geometric shapes of the hanging lantern, bedside table cube, modular wall shelf, and picture frame.

◄ COMFORTABLY CASUAL
Soft colors, natural materials, and simplicity make for a cozy room. The very popular color scheme of light blues and greens creates a casual feel that suggests a country cottage or mountain cabin. Cotton fabrics, a wooden headboard, and a hanging plant continue the theme. Sheer drapery panels hanging from a decorative pewter rod make the room feel larger and more airy.

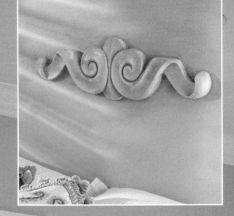

ELEGANTLY TRADITIONAL Traditional décor has a more subtle and luxurious feel than other styles. The key to creating this style is to focus on the decorative details. Start with a neutral color scheme. Painting the headboard the same classic gold hue as the walls and then glazing it keeps the room open and light. This simple headboard, constructed of plywood and lumber, gains elegance with the addition of a decorative wood appliqué. Traditional white plantation shutters and an antiqued bronze bedside lamp enhance the formal atmosphere of the room.

For instructions on making all three headboards, plus the Contemporary bedside table cube and modular wall shelf, visit LowesCreativeIdeas.com, click on Archive, select "One Bedroom Three Ways," and scroll down to the links to how-to directions.

BEFORE Having put most of their efforts into remodeling the rooms the family used together, these homeowners had neglected their own bedroom. It provided a place to sleep but lacked visual interest, storage space, and—the wife's particular desire—a place to read. Furnishings were spare and uncoordinated. The only lighting in the room came from small wall lamps on either side of the bed.

AFTER Now bookcases flank a comfortable window seat. Trimmed with crown moulding that continues around the room, the built-ins are the focal point. Because the husband is an accomplished woodworker, he was able to build customized units, so they provide storage and display space and the coveted place for reading. The aqua and taupe color scheme, new Roman shades and bed linens, and attractive lamps add warmth and softness to the room.

thedetails

building a bookcase wall

A BUILT-IN UNIT like the one shown here can dramatically alter a room. If you have a suitable wall, you can hire a contractor to build custom cabinets, shelves, and a window seat for you. But if you have good carpentry skills, you may wish to do it yourself. The explanation here gives general guidelines for the project. This bookcase and window seat wall was built from scratch, but you may be able to start with purchased unfinished wood cabinets and bookcases.

• **Plan the unit.** The base cabinets and window seat should be roughly 2 feet deep, and the bookcases should be 12 inches deep. A good height for the base cabinets is 36 inches; 20 inches will work well for the window seat. Draw a general plan to facilitate construction.

• **Build the cabinets and shelves.** Cut medium-density fiberboard (MDF) plywood sheets to form the base-cabinet and bookcase frames. Drill evenly spaced holes in the interior sides of bookcases (a template will help align the holes) to hold the adjustable shelves. Assemble the frames on either side of the window. Cut base-cabinet tops out of MDF, using a rounded edge or a ¾-inch half-round trim for a finished look. Install them.

• **Build the window seat.** Build a frame for the window seat out of 2 × 4 lumber. Attach vertical 1 × 4 strips on the front of the seat at evenly spaced intervals. From MDF, make front panels (flat or beveled) for the

seat and for the base-cabinet doors. Attach the seat panels to the 1 × 4 vertical members. Cut a window-seat top out of MDF.

• **Add moulding and paint.** Measure, cut, and install crown moulding around the top of the cabinets and ceiling edges for a finished look. Fill all nail holes with wood putty, then sand and prime all surfaces. Let dry, sand, and paint.

• **Finish assembly.** Install the base-cabinet doors and hardware. Secure the window seat to the frame with a piano hinge. Finally, cut shelves from scrap material, prime and paint them, and install them in the bookcases.

For information on how to install crown moulding around the top of cabinets and ceiling edges, go to Lowes.com and search with the keyword "moulding," then click on "Installing Moulding" under Project Center.

how to choose a ceiling color

YOU CAN GIVE NEW LIFE TO A ROOM simply by painting the ceiling. Think of it as a fifth wall, an opportunity to add color or alter the mood of the room. To judge the impact a color will have, test it on a portion of the ceiling adjacent to the wall. You can increase the effect of the ceiling color by applying it to the top 10 to 12 inches of the wall, as in the simulations shown here.

• **FOR PEACEFUL SETTINGS,** use the same color on the wall and ceiling in different intensities (right). Neutrals, blues, violets, and greens are the most relaxing colors to work with.

• **GIVE ENERGY TO A ROOM** by painting the ceiling in a color complementary to the one on the walls. Use a combination such as red and green, blue and orange, or yellow and violet (below left), and be careful not to make the colors too intense.

• **TO LIFT A CEILING,** select a pale tint of a cool hue such as green or blue (below center). These colors visually recede.

• **TO CREATE AN INTIMATE SPACE** or to lower a ceiling, try a dark, warm tone—red, rust, or brown—that appears to come closer (below right). The ceiling should be darker than the walls.

American Tradition, Churchill Hotel Lace #7003-17, satin

American Tradition, Homestead Resort Pumpkin #3003-6B, flat

American Tradition, Lavender Escape #4002-7B, flat

American Tradition, Lake Breeze #5007-7B, flat

American Tradition, Molera Vaquero Red #2001-7A, flat

American Tradition, Churchill Hotel Lace #7003-17, satin

do-it-yourself headboards

Simple materials and easy steps create a new look.

As one of the most visible elements in a bedroom, the headboard can be a major focal point. Change your bedroom's look with one of these stylish designs you can make yourself.

▽**DAZZLING DIAMONDS** This simple-to-make headboard adds color and dimension to any bedroom. Cut a sheet of medium-density fiberboard (MDF) to fit the width of the bed. Sand the edges and apply two coats of a lighter-color paint to the front surface. Then mark a 12 × 16-inch diamond pattern, beginning at the center of the board and working toward the edges. Tape off the diamonds with painter's tape and, with a sponge brush, fill in alternate diamonds with two coats of a darker paint. When it's dry, tape an outline along all diamond edges and fill in the outline with a gold glaze. Dot with gold-painted dowel plugs. Gold-painted moulding, drapery rods, and finials adorn the sides.

△**LOUVERED DOORS** This unique headboard showcases a pair of ordinary louvered bifold doors and crown moulding. Start with a piece of 66¼ × 48-inch plywood. Measure 45 inches down from the top of the doors and cut them off; you will use the top section for the headboard. Stain the plywood and the doors. Attach the doors to the plywood, leaving 3¼ inches of plywood showing at the top and sides; the door bottoms will be flush with the bottom edge of the plywood. Attach mitered crown moulding around the headboard for a finished touch. For detailed instructions, go to Lowes.com/greenbed.

▽**LATTICE** A sheet of maple lattice adds depth and texture to this bright red headboard. Cut an opening in a sheet of ¾-inch plywood and attach the lattice panel to the back. Add a 2 × 4 support to each side. Attach cove moulding along the inside edge of the frame and trim the exposed plywood edges with iron-on veneer. For detailed instructions, visit LowesCreativeIdeas.com, click on "Archive," and select "Room and Board" under Bedroom.

CHILDREN'S BEDROOMS should reflect their ages and interests. But since both change rapidly, design the room to accommodate that growth. You'll want to allow lots of room for young children to play and incorporate a study area for school-age children and teens. Use colors that are warm and patterns that are interesting, but neither should be overstimulating. And always provide good storage to organize the myriad toys, books, clothes, and memorabilia kids accumulate.

BEFORE Two sisters share this high-ceilinged room, which had a great window and plenty of floor space but little else. The south-facing arched window begged for some kind of treatment, and the stark bunk beds took up the only uninterrupted wall in the room.

AFTER A subtle floral bas-relief and light pleated curtains now frame the window and draw attention to the great view outside. Inside, the view is also captivating. Warm peach walls and colorfully painted furniture enliven the room. Placing the bunk bed on the diagonal not only creates an interesting composition but also makes room for a bureau and desk along the wall. Slipcovers stitched from an old quilt, bedspreads made from cotton-duck shower curtains, and puffy bolsters created from a translucent curtain panel soften the look of the metal bed frame.

▲ **ARTFUL DISPLAY** Shallow shelves are ideal for showing off children's artwork and favorite photos. These are just inexpensive "wiggle moulding" (used to support corrugated-metal roofing) and strands of colorful glass beads on lengths of simple 2 × 2 lumber. Clever picture frames are made from sheets of acrylic held together with plastic clips.

BEFORE An attic room was home to old furniture that had nowhere else to go. Its white walls and plywood floor were a blank canvas for a makeover.

AFTER Bold colors make the high-ceilinged room come alive, creating a great atmosphere for a young boy. Paint is a fun and inexpensive floor-covering solution. To keep the look playful, the homeowners painted the end wall with two tones of blue topped with a glazing medium, creating the look of denim squares. Wall cupboards and simple wire cubes provide great storage for clothes and toys.

▶ CHALKBOARD MAGIC
Blackboard paint transforms plain cupboard doors into practical surfaces for a budding artist to test his craft. Bright yellow-orange trim outlines the doors dramatically.

READY-MADE DÉCOR
For a simple way to add decorative touches to a room, look for coordinated ensembles of matching decorative items, such as:

- wallpaper borders
- night-lights
- three-dimensional wall art
- paint stamps
- switch plates

#1 imagination station

A DEDICATED WORKTABLE where children can paint, glue, and crayon to their hearts' content keeps the mess in one place. With adjustable sawhorse legs, the table can grow with your children.

STEP 1: Cut the plywood to the desired length and width and sand the edges until they are completely smooth.

STEP 2: Prime the board, including the edges, and allow it to dry.

STEP 3: Apply the base coat; allow it to dry. Apply a second coat if needed. Once the base coat is dry, use a contrasting color to paint large polka dots. Let the paint dry. With a third color, paint smaller dots within the large ones. Allow them to dry.

STEP 4: Extend the sawhorse legs to the desired height of the table.

STEP 5: Place the tabletop on the floor, painted side down. Place the sawhorses on top of the board, upside down.

STEP 6: Using ¾-inch screws, attach the sawhorses to the board through existing holes in the sawhorses. To protect the floor, attach felt pads to the bottoms of the sawhorse legs. Turn the table upright.

#2 rotating art gallery

SET UP A GALLERY along one wall of a playroom or child's bedroom that can display each new masterpiece. Install a curtain rod at a level suitable for people viewing the artwork. Add coordinating curtain rings with clips to hold pieces of all sizes.

Lowe's Shopping List

Materials
- 1 (4 feet × 8 feet) sheet of ¾-inch-thick plywood
- 2 yellow sawhorses
- primer
- purple paint (American Tradition, Berries Galore #4001-10B, semi-gloss)
- red paint (American Tradition, Oh So Red #1009-1, semi-gloss)
- yellow paint (American Tradition, Golden Flame #3002-1A, semi-gloss)
- sandpaper
- ¾-inch felt pads

Tools
- drill/driver
- screwdriver
- paintbrushes

Skill level: Beginner
Rough cost estimate: $140*
Rough time estimate: 1 day

*Does not include applicable taxes, which vary by market, or the cost of tools.

great closets

THE BEST WAY to ensure a relaxing atmosphere in any bedroom is to hold down the clutter. With a large walk-in closet, it's easy, but even smaller, 24-inch-deep ones can be easily organized with the many systems available at Lowe's.

▶ HIDDEN STORAGE

Use base or stacked units with drawers to store folded items, such as undergarments, shirts, and shorts. Keep track of socks by rolling them into a drawer organizer. To quickly pair the day's attire with matching accessories, use a jewelry insert in a closet drawer to hold each grouping. The top of a base unit can serve as a dressing table or provide extra storage.

▲ HANGING STORAGE

Figure out what clothing you need to hang and install just enough rods to accommodate those items. You'll want to reserve as much space as possible for other kinds of storage. Separate pants, shirts, jackets, and dresses and hang them in groups—you'll find it easier to locate clothes quickly. Hang seasonal items together.

◀ OPEN STORAGE

Shelves in a stacked or corner unit, or in a hanging unit if you have extra rod space, keep everyday items right where you need them. They are great for folded clothes, handbags, shoes, hats, and storage boxes.

For a more in-depth look at how to bring order to every room of your house, look for Lowe's *Creative Ideas for Organizing Your Home*, a 128-page book available at Lowe's.

◄ HOOKS Don't underestimate the power of a hook. Use one to hang dressing gowns and robes, or a series to hang jackets, pants, belts—anything that can hold its shape without a hanger. A double hook provides extra storage in a narrow space. A telescoping valet hook puts freshly ironed shirts at the front of the closet. It is also useful as short-term storage for items recently picked up from the dry cleaners.

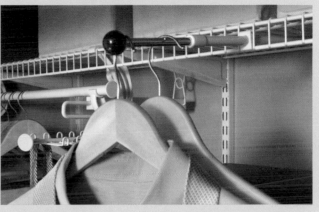

▼ CHILD'S CLOSET A versatile closet system with shelves, rods, and a closed cabinet offers everything you need to store a child's clothes and spare bedding. Canvas bins on shelves make perfect toy boxes. Keep height in mind when designing a child's closet. This one incorporates both open and closed storage at varying levels to help the parents control what their child can access.

▲ BABY'S CLOSET A standard closet with sliding doors can become a diaper-changing alcove. Remove the doors and install a changing table with drawers and shelves below for diapers, accessories, and tiny clothes.

bathrooms

AFTER KITCHENS, BATHROOMS ARE THE MOST

REMODELED rooms in the house—and for good reason. We

all want stylish, inviting bathrooms that function well.

Exceptional bathrooms result from a good layout,

high-quality fixtures, appropriate lighting, attractive finishes,

and accessibility for everyone. Decorative details

enhance the look.

Look through this chapter for great examples—

from elaborate master home spas to charming powder

rooms to budget-minded kids' bathrooms of ways to use space

to great advantage, innovative products, and the kinds

of details that set both a style and a mood.

FREE BATH PROJECT PLANNER

Go to Lowes.com/BathPlanner to download this free planner. With tips, trends, ideas, and inspiration, it will help you create the bath of your dreams.

A gracious bathroom replaced an unfinished section of the basement in this makeover. See pages 102–103 for more information.

AT ITS BEST, the master bathroom is a spa-like haven that promises relaxation and rejuvenation. To make it really inviting, focus on the amenities you particularly enjoy. A deep soaking tub with jets is worth the investment if you love a long bath. If possible, surround it with windows to give you a view of the outdoors. Or, if you rarely use the tub, dedicate space for a large shower stall with multiple spa-style jet sprays. Add separate sinks and grooming stations if two people will use the bathroom at the same time.

 The bones of the old bathroom were fine, but the homeowner wanted something more distinctive with a better layout and more storage. Ceramic tile and a motif of curves keyed the sophisticated approach.

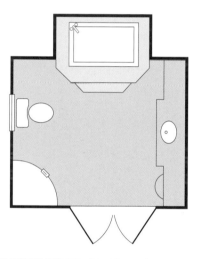

▼ **CONTOURED ELEGANCE** Even the toilet, with its rounded edges, adds style to this well-designed bathroom. Above the toilet, a glass-block window is easy to clean and offers privacy without a shade or curtain.

AFTER The arch above the tub, an interesting architectural feature, became the main focal point of the new bathroom. Reflected in the large mirror that covers the wall above the vanity, curved lines are prominent in fixtures throughout the room. Not only pleasing to the eye, the curves soften the strong grout lines of the ceramic tile work. Mixing colors, sizes, and textures of tiles creates visual interest and adds another element of drama. To create a masculine atmosphere, the homeowner selected a rich brown and black color scheme.

▶ **SHOWER IN THE ROUND** A new circular shower in one corner echoes the curve of the arch above the bath alcove. Its tempered-glass doors make both left- and right-hand entry possible. The shower controls are conveniently located in a column between the glass panels. The shower has four body-massage jets.

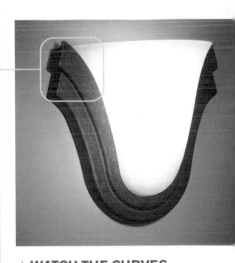

▲ **WATCH THE CURVES** The sculpted curves of the wall sconces contrast with the squareness of the tiles while also repeating the line of the arch above the tub. Good lighting is imperative above a vanity. To learn more about lighting options, see pages 52–53.

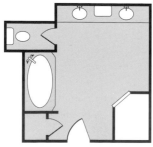

NEW ADDITION These homeowners added a master bath to their home that combines the best of two worlds. Asian-inspired design elements and calming colors evoke Eastern sensibilities, while contemporary fixtures and accessories lend Western convenience to the room. A preexisting exterior stone wall forms a textural backdrop for an elegant bath nook. It also serves as the inspiration for the natural materials and earthy hues on other surfaces.

▶ LUXURIOUS SHOWERS

In the corner shower stall, dual showerheads spray water from adjacent walls. For easy maintenance, the homeowners selected a subtle green-gray tile that resembles slate for the shower floor and walls.

▲ ASIAN LOOK

A long vanity and counter gain sophisticated character with the addition of a cherry cabinet separating the elegant above-counter sinks. Black Asian-style knobs and pulls evoke the look of antique Chinese medicine chests, while sleek wall-mounted faucets add a modern counterpoint. Above the vanity, the earth colors of a natural quartz countertop and a slate backsplash blend well with the natural stone on the nearby wall. Bowl-shaped sconces above each iron mirror mimic the shape of the sinks.

BEFORE Back-to-back bathrooms—a half bath off the master bedroom and a full bath off the hallway—were tiled in dated colors and were too small to be comfortable. The couple came up with a plan that involved relocating hall and bedroom closets to create two full baths: one for him and one for her. They kept costs down by using existing plumbing, adding lines only for a shower in his bath. Most of their budget went toward tiling, in a mix of neutral colors for a long-lasting style.

AFTER **HERS** The hall bath was hers, but because of its location, the remodel was designed to double as a guest bath. She selected 12-inch-square gray and white marble floor tiles to give the bathroom a luxurious feel. Six-inch ceramic tiles in a complementary tone were laid diagonally in the tub surround. Soft green walls promote relaxation, while white plantation shutters provide light and privacy in this simple, clean design.

▲ **CHARMING VANITY** An inexpensive white 30-inch vanity provides storage without dominating the space. An off-white solid-surface top and brushed-chrome hardware continue the clean look. The white oval mirror, flanked by sconces, adds a feminine touch.

▼ **HIDDEN STORAGE** Two 15 × 30-inch unfinished wall cabinets were painted white and recessed into the wall to create storage for linens and bath accessories.

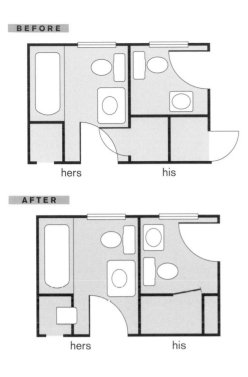

BEFORE

hers   his

AFTER

hers   his

AFTER HIS Since his bathroom opened to the master bedroom, it warranted a more dramatic focal point: an attractive, generously sized shower stall. Earth tones and simple lines lend it a warm but masculine feel. He chose four coordinating tiles to create an attractive pattern: 12-inch-square ceramic for the walls, 2-inch-square tumbled marble for the floor, 6-inch-square ceramic for the ceiling, and a decorative tumbled-marble band made of 12-inch strips of mosaic tiles on a woven background. A frameless glass door opens up the room and also allows the tile detail to be seen from outside. Chosen to fit the small space, a pedestal sink with a polished chrome faucet keeps the look clean-lined and simple.

▶ **DUAL CONTROL** Single-handle levers control the two showerheads, which can be used one at a time or simultaneously. A combination of an 8-inch-diameter showerhead on the ceiling and a standard showerhead in the wall creates a relaxing spa-like experience.

▶ **HANDY NOOK** A wall niche in the shower holds soap and shampoo.

Vintage style sets the theme for this makeover.

BEFORE Blue can be a great color in a bathroom, but these homeowners thought the baby-blue sink, tub, and toilet were a bit too much. With the intention of keeping the same floor plan but changing all fixtures and finishes, they tore out the yellow tile and blue fixtures and went to work remaking their small master bathroom.

AFTER They started with the architecture. The homeowners favored vintage style and knew they wanted a neutral palette. By running a tall beadboard wainscot around the walls and using deep wooden trim for the baseboards, chair rail, and crown moulding, they established a Victorian theme. Next they created a great-looking floor pattern using 12-inch-square marble tile on the diagonal with a 9-inch-wide border, which made the room look more expansive. The walls were painted a warm chocolate brown to match the darkest flecks in the marble, and the wainscot was painted white to lighten the room.

◀ BATH SURROUND
To give the simple 5-foot-long tub surround a more sophisticated look and coordinate it with the floor tile, 4-inch beige matte-finish tiles are set on the diagonal. Square niches recessed into the wall hold soap and shampoo.

▲ RICH DETAILS A traditional pedestal sink with a deck wide enough to handle soap and other bathroom accessories contributes to the Victorian effect. When the homeowners found a mirror and sconces in the right style but the wrong color, they painted them a deep chocolate brown to match the mirror. For a bit of ambience, a dimmer switch was installed to allow different lighting levels. With limited closed storage, a large basket provides an attractive container for towels and tissue.

◀ PRACTICAL LUXURY

A walk-in shower is ideal for busy mornings. And when there is time to spare, body jets make bathing a luxurious experience. The same blue and white tile design above the tub is used here, and the chrome edging of the frameless glass shower door coordinates with other metallic finishes in the room.

▲ SMART STORAGE

At one end of the jetted bath, a built-in nook with water-resistant solid-surface shelves adds a punch of color. In addition to the cabinets in the vanity, there's storage in the linen closet between the tub and shower and in a cabinet above the toilet.

NEW ADDITION When these homeowners had the opportunity to add a master bathroom onto their home, they focused on two priorities: creating a place to relax and maximizing storage. They succeeded in creating a luxurious retreat on a tight budget through planning and by taking advantage of in-stock products. To keep the style contemporary and simple, they chose a three-color palette: bright white for the tile walls and floor, denim blue for the solid-surface countertop and decorative accents, and a soft cinnamon finish for the wooden vanity. Above each mirror is a fixture with adjustable lights.

planning for privacy

Here are several strategies for creating a private space.

You should always feel that you can relax and be comfortable in the privacy of your bathroom. But you may want to add special elements, especially if a bathroom is used by more than one person at a time or if it has low windows. With careful planning, you can incorporate features that make your bathroom as private as possible.

▶ **TOILET ENCLOSURES**
There are several ways to minimize the visibility of a toilet or hide it altogether. If you have a large enough space, you can enclose it in its own water closet, using a swing-out or pocket door (right). In an open layout, set the toilet in the least visible position, either tucked behind the door as it opens or between the vanity and the faucet end of the tub. You can also hide it behind a low wall, in which you incorporate shelving for storage.

▼ **WINDOWS** Rather than cover windows with blinds or curtains, consider opaqued glass, as in the wheelchair-accessible bath below.

▲ **TUB AND SHOWER SOLUTIONS** In many bathrooms, tubs or shower stalls are designed to take center stage. But if privacy is an issue, locating the tub or shower on the same wall as the door will make it less visible. For more privacy, use some kind of screen—permanent or movable— to separate the bathing area from the rest of the bathroom. If you prefer to use a glass enclosure, select translucent glass or glass block (above). Another option is to hang a curtain, either from a rod around the tub or from a track on the ceiling.

universal design for easy living

Everybody can benefit when accessibility is planned into the makeover.

WITH ANY REMODEL, good accessibility, ease of use, and safety are features you want to build in. When you integrate universal design into your plans, you create a space that can accommodate both current and any changing needs of your family and friends. Universal design is about environments and products that make life easier for as many individuals as possible, regardless of age or ability.

Consider these top ten features of universal design for your next remodeling project:

1. The first floor needs an accessible bedroom, bathroom, kitchen, living area, and laundry room. Hallways should be 42 inches wide, doorways at least 32 inches wide. Swing-clear hinges can be installed on existing doors to widen the openings.

2. Handrails should be installed on both sides of all exterior and interior stairways. For interior stairways, the banister should be installed 1½ inches from the wall and fastened securely into studs.

3. A walk-in/roll-in shower is necessary in a first-floor bath. Important features include scald-control faucets, a handheld adjustable showerhead, and a portable shower seat or bathtub seat.

4. Grab bars must be installed in shower/tub areas for safety. Be sure walls near toilets and showers are strong enough for the grab bars.

5. Accessible storage, such as multiple-height and adjustable-height shelves, is important in closets and cabinets.

DOUBLE DOORS, an unimpeded threshold, several grab bars, and a handheld sprayer all make this shower fully accessible.

A RAISED DISHWASHER limits bending, for pain-free loading and unloading.

A WALL OVEN located lower than standard height is easier for short adults as well as those in wheelchairs. It has rollout shelves that slide forward for better access.

AN UNDERCOUNTER MICROWAVE makes moving heavy dishes safer. It's also within anyone's reach.

6. Lighting features include outlets and switches with dimmers located 18 to 48 inches from the floor. Exterior walkways, porches, halls, and stairs should be well lit.

7. Easy-grip controls are needed throughout the house. These include lever handles on doors and faucets, D-shaped pulls, rocker-panel light switches, touch-pad controls, and larger-size controls.

8. Select easy-access appliances such as a front-loading washer and dryer, side-by-side refrigerator, elevated dishwasher, and electric range with front controls. Also choose large-print, color-contrasting controls.

9. Safe flooring features include low or no thresholds (for heights of ¼ inch or more, install a beveled threshold strip), surfaces that are nonslip and nonglare, and low-pile carpets or rugs.

10. Safety devices, including smoke detectors, night-lights, temperature-limiting mixer valves (anti-scald devices), and carbon monoxide detectors are vital to any home.

WITH WORK SURFACES OF MULTIPLE HEIGHTS, anyone can help out in the kitchen.

POWDER ROOMS AND GUEST BATHS

POWDER ROOMS AND GUEST BATHS are great places to have fun with design. With the wide variety of bathroom appointments available, you can turn even the smallest space into a true gem. Choose one specific decorating style and stick with a simple color scheme. Consider making a guest bathroom one that can be used by anyone, with amenities such as stainless-steel grab bars in the tub area and alongside the toilet.

BEFORE The wallpaper was too busy and clashed with the dingy green tile, which had begun to chip. The homeowners also recognized that the old bathtub, beyond any simple repair, was rarely used.

AFTER While nothing moved, everything changed. The old pedestal sink was given new elegance with a serene monochromatic background of white beadboard wainscot, white floor tiles, and soft blue paint. A brushed-nickel faucet was selected to complement the silver matte grout and wall color. The framed mirror and decorative light fixture are also carefully planned details that reinforce the simple cottage style. Because the vintage toilet tank and bowl could not be salvaged in one piece, the homeowners replaced the fixture with a taller one that coordinates with the sink. And after an old and underused second doorway to the right of the sink was removed, there was room to install a towel bar and table.

◀ CUSTOM STALL

Preferring a shower that could be used by old and young guests alike, the homeowners replaced the cast-iron tub with an angled custom shower stall. The decorative tile work combines a warm beige tile with a 4-inch version of the white tile that was used on the floor.

CABINET DOORS With a little modification, 72-inch-tall plantation shutters were made into cabinet doors for the linen closet. Mimicking the blinds on the window, the doors continue the room's cottage theme.

BEFORE An outdated hallway bathroom accommodated guests, but the space was inefficient. Built-in shelving was inadequate and difficult to access, and the vanity and sink were too small. The homeowners wanted a modernized room with style.

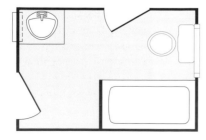

BEFORE

AFTER Sometimes the only thing to do with a bad floor plan is to start over. In this case, the homeowners chose to move a wall and door several feet out, relocate the tub to the far end of the room, position the vanity against the longer wall, and move the toilet to the opposite corner. The new bathroom, strikingly sophisticated, marries traditional and contemporary elements for a clean, urban style.

AFTER

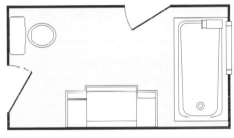

◀ **CONTRASTS THAT WORK** The visual focal point of the room, the furniture-style vanity, was created with a 21-inch-deep base cabinet centered between two 18-inch-deep drawer units. Their dark cherry wood provides a high contrast to the stark white solid-surface countertop, sink, and ceramic tile, while the round curves of the modern brushed-nickel faucet, finger pulls, and wall sconces balance the straight lines of the traditional cabinets. To offset the dramatic contrast, the homeowners selected a soft sage green for the walls. Trimming the mirror with 4-inch cherry moulding pulls the whole look together beautifully.

▲ **A BIT OF NOSTALGIA**
Resembling the intricate tile work seen in many bathrooms of the 1940s and 1950s, the graphic floor pattern adds interest to the room. It pairs nostalgic hexagonal tiles in white with up-to-date 1-inch-square white and light gray tiles, which are mounted on 12-inch-square sheets for quick, easy installation.

BEFORE An unfinished basement was an obvious place to add much needed guest quarters in an older home. The couple also wanted a bathroom that would accommodate a tall family member who was moving in.

AFTER The desire for low maintenance and for good ergonomics set the design tone of this bathroom (also shown on pages 84–85). The countertops were built at 33½ inches high, and a 16½-inch-high toilet was special-ordered. Ivory cabinetry, ginger-colored countertops, and taupe walls and flooring combine a sophisticated look with easy care. The contemporary pearl-nickel pulls on the drawers and cabinets are not only stylish but provide easy access because of their simple grip. Well-placed towel bars and rings keep towels within reach. Cabinet towers flank the vanity area, providing lots of space for linens and toiletries.

► ROOMY SHOWER The shower is oversized, with a wide glass door for easy access. The 12-inch beige tiles on the walls are easy to clean because of minimal grout lines.

◄ HIDDEN HAMPER At the base of each cabinet tower, a slide-out hamper provides plenty of room for towels and dirty clothes. It's details like this that make a well-designed bathroom a delight.

▼ CLEAN LINES Though the room is large, its design called for only one stretch of countertop. So the couple splurged on a solid-surface counter with a white molded sink—easy to clean, with no sink lip to trap dirt.

little space, big style

Have fun with a powder room.

A powder room is a great place to surprise your guests with a decorating style that is uniquely yours. Usually tucked away to the side of an entry or under a stairwell, a powder room does not have to adhere to the style of your home. It can be traditional, contemporary, or completely playful. The photos here illustrate three ways to set a style using different wall treatments, fixtures, and accessories. A few well-chosen decorative details complete the look.

◀ JAZZY TRADITIONAL

Fusing 1940s glamour with today's multi-carat glitz, this retro powder room is high on style without sacrificing practicality. The European-style vanity takes up no floor space and sports its own towel bar. Its brushed-nickel faucet complements the shimmery bronze dots on the wallpaper and the antique-reproduction mirror. Clear prisms on the chandelier (below) and beaded-glass shades on the sconces add a bit of over-the-top sparkle.

▶ **COLORFUL CASUAL** By painting vibrant vertical stripes on the wall, you can imbue the room with a sense of whimsy that puts your guests at ease. The simple white vanity and countertop are versatile enough to suit any style, and they balance the boldest of color palettes. Fun chrome pendant lights provide good task lighting. Continuing the playful theme, the mirror frame is decorated with nickel upholstery brads.

◀ **NATURALLY CONTEMPORARY**

Geometric lines and smooth curves bring a quality of cutting-edge design to this sophisticated space. The grass-cloth wall covering, which gives a natural, almost rustic texture, is hung horizontally so as to widen the room visually. The rich wooden cabinet contributes a more earthy ambience, while the frosted-glass sink and vanity door panel add cool, polished touches.

FOR YOUNG CHILDREN, the bathroom is a fun place to splash and play at the end of the day. It should be colorful, light-hearted, and safe. As children grow, their needs change. When you design your children's bathroom to accommodate their growth, you won't have to remodel it over and over again. Limit the most child-oriented features in the room to finishes and accessories that are easy and inexpensive to change, such as colorful shower curtains and accessories. Here are four makeovers that serve children now and will remain appropriate in future years.

BEFORE This bathroom functioned well when the homeowners' child was young, but it fell short when he grew old enough to use it on his own. There was no mirror or anywhere for storing towels and toiletries. His parents didn't want to remake the room, but they did want to make it serviceable for a 9-year-old.

AFTER Do-it yourself projects added style and function to this bath. Each feature was designed very simply, with traditional details to match the room. First, with lumber and wooden trim, the homeowners built and painted a footstool that allows their son to reach the sink easily. Next, using wooden moulding, decorative corner blocks, and a piece of lumber, they made a mirror to fit between the sink and light fixture. Finally, they created a stylish storage unit that fits in the narrow space between the sink and tub. With these few simple additions, the son now finds his bathroom "really cool."

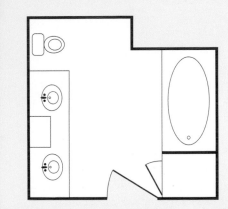

FRESH START Pattern creates whimsy in this bathroom for a pair of preschoolers. Large and small mint-green dots are scattered playfully around the walls. Made of painted cork mats, the dots were affixed to the walls with a small amount of adhesive so they can be removed when the children are older. The cork mats are also used as decorative accents behind the towel bars. Painted dowel plugs trim the corners of each wood-framed mirror, and green wooden knobs on the cabinetry continue the polka-dot theme.

▶ **TIMELESS ELEGANCE**
The white double-sink vanity, with its beadboard, vertical rope accents, decorative feet, and tile backsplash, will look good—and function well for the girls—for many years.

BEFORE A 1960s brown and white bathroom with a single sink and limited storage was a challenge for growing boys. The parents wanted a more inviting space that the twins could both use at the same time and that would suit them through their teens.

AFTER Island-inspired textures and patterns transformed the bathroom into a masculine retreat with a worldly flair. The vinyl grass cloth sets a tropical tone for the room; as a bonus, the strippable, scrubbable wallcovering will withstand the occasional water fight. The ceiling was painted an olive green to complement the walls, and rich burgundy-colored cabinetry and bright white trim add handsome contrasts. The homeowners enhanced the rustic style by laying stone tiles in a running bond pattern, with the grout matched to the creamy tan countertop. Leaving the toilet, tub, and tile surround in place made this stylish makeover affordable.

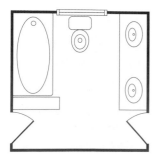

▲ **DOUBLE-DUTY CEILING FIXTURE** While recessed lights provide good task lighting above the vanity, a ceiling fixture with an oil-rubbed bronze finish and alabaster glass globe offers more subtle general lighting. The classic fixture hides its double function as a bath fan.

▲ **TEXTURE AND PATTERN** A palm-tree shower curtain and woven wooden shades reinforce the island theme.

▲ **TIDY STORAGE** The two mirrors above the vanity swing out to reveal a place for each boy to store his own toiletries.

▲ **NATURAL STYLE** Bronze lever faucets, with easy-grip handles for large or small hands, are well suited to a masculine room.

BEFORE A pink bathroom was hardly a teenage boy's ideal. Fortunately, the existing layout, with its two sinks, long vanity, and large shower stall, was adequate. The goal was an updated and appropriate bathroom.

AFTER Deep earth tones are more appropriate for a young man and are more forgiving of the grass and dirt that follow a teenager's clothes and equipment home. The makeover started with a reddish-brown ceramic floor tile that dictated the rest of the color scheme: a rich coffee color for the walls, with white on the trim and shelving units to match the woodwork in the rest of the house. The most ingenious solution for this remodel was the new shower stall. Rather than replacing the old pink wall tiles, the homeowners removed them, then installed a three-piece white shower unit that fit the space perfectly. To its left, they reworked existing wall cabinets into more easily accessible open shelves for towels and bath accessories.

▲ **FURNITURE QUALITY** A deep-mocha-colored cherrywood vanity completed the earth-tone scheme. Its texture and detailing suggest the look of an antique chest, perfect for a masculine bathroom. Having saved money on the shower, the homeowners were able to splurge on a solid-surface countertop with two seamless integrated white sinks. Its color and edging detail complement the room's style.

Recessed lights and open shelves provide a clean, architectural effect.

utility
spaces

WITH CAREFUL PLANNING and a little ingenuity, you can turn a dark and dusty corner into an inviting place to launder clothes, carry out projects, or pursue hobbies. The efficient appliances and storage systems now available can help you bring an entirely new look to a useful space.

You might convert a room to a laundry or hobby space, or appropriate part of the garage or basement. In many homes, a corner of the kitchen makes an ideal spot for a laundry center. If the area you are working with seems inadequate, look for ways to change the floor plan. Maybe you can annex an adjoining closet or tuck shelves between wall studs.

Look through the following pages for exciting examples of how other homeowners turned their utility areas into lighter, brighter spaces.

An underused closet becomes a multipurpose craft station that everyone in the family can enjoy (see page 124).

DOING LAUNDRY might become a favorite activity if you could sort, fold, and iron clothes in a fresh, stylish space that you enjoy being in. The makeovers shown here provide plenty of inspiration for developing a laundry room that is as inviting as it is efficient.

To create these laundry rooms, the homeowners remodeled existing spaces—with great results. New cabinetry, paint or paneling, and handsome flooring catch the eye. Behind their good looks, these rooms are well equipped. Their energy-efficient appliances will eventually pay for themselves in utility savings, and attractive new storage keeps linens and cleaning supplies within easy reach.

FRESH START Even the dog has a place to wash in this streamlined laundry area. When the homeowners decided it was time to remodel their old laundry room, they took the opportunity to create a dedicated place to bathe their family pets. The room was then designed to separate the cutting-edge appliances from the open shower. Dark, easy-to-clean ceramic tile disguises dog hair and dirt in this high-traffic area. Drywall was installed over the existing cinder blocks and painted a fresh green to liven up the space. And plenty of closed storage, hanging space, and some hardworking accessories combine to lighten the laundry load.

▶ **PET SMART** With a low, detachable nozzle, easy-to-reach knobs, and a stabilizing grab bar, this shower is a hassle-free area for the kids to wash the dog. It's also spacious enough to water large plants, rinse muddy shoes, or drip-dry delicates from two hooks placed up above on the wall.

◀ HANG 'EM HIGH

A rod beneath a shelf keeps newly laundered clothes wrinkle-free. A second rod to the right of the sink provides more hanging space.

▶ WAIST LEVEL

Steel pedestals raise the front-load washer and dryer, making it easier to load and unload clothes. A drawer in each platform offers storage as well.

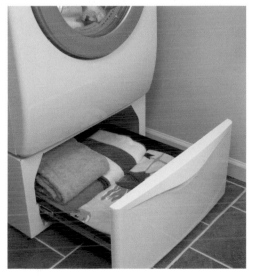

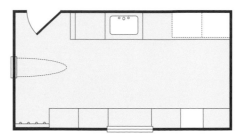

BEFORE Mismatched cabinetry, cold cinder-block walls, and poor lighting defined this poorly used basement before the homeowners decided to give it a makeover. They wanted a space that combined the laundry with storage for art materials.

AFTER The basement laundry has a brighter disposition, with sage green walls, white cabinets, and sunny yellow countertops. And now there is a place for everything, making it an efficient and fun place to work. New cabinets and energy-efficient appliances were an obvious addition, but a real benefit comes from the pegboard behind the countertop, which was nailed onto furring strips that cover the old cinder block. It provides plenty of options for hanging craft tools and supplies.

◄ AMPLE STORAGE On the wall across from the laundry area, freestanding modular cabinets and cubbies offer plenty of convenient storage. For complete instructions on making the cubbies, visit LowesCreativeIdeas.com, click on "Archive," and select "Open Storage Cubbies" under Step-by-Step Projects.

► IRONING STATION A wall cabinet hides an ironing station, close at hand when it's needed and out of the way when it's not.

ONE OF THE MOST REWARDING

spaces to make over is the garage. It's the best location for major storage, and when well organized, it also provides ample room for a variety of activities. The real challenge is getting past all the clutter to envision something new. The garage remodels on the following pages prove that anything is possible with good planning and materials.

PLANNING A WORKSHOP When you consider converting at least part of your garage to a workshop, you need to plan for big projects as well as heavy materials and tools. Think of sturdy work surfaces, a dedicated place for every tool, and a mobile unit that can be pulled into the middle of the room for large projects. There are many different component systems at various prices; check Lowe's to find the one that's right for your workshop.

LAUNCHING A GARAGE MAKEOVER

No matter what you're planning for your garage, start with these three steps.

1. Clear out everything you no longer use and get rid of the discards. Hold a garage sale, recycle, give to a charity. Be sure to dispose of hazardous materials properly.
2. Clean the space thoroughly.
3. Plan storage for the items you need to keep. Organize it all into categories: things you use regularly, things you use seasonally, and things you have put aside for the future. Then visit Lowe's to find the right storage solution for each category (see pages 120–121).

BEFORE While this garage was large enough to accumulate clutter and still leave room for the cars, it was not living up to its potential. Garden tools had a place on the walls, but everything else was jumbled in corners and piled haphazardly on the floor.

AFTER Once these homeowners had cleared the clutter and cleaned the space, they put up beadboard and hardboard paneling. Hardboard is a little more costly than gypsum drywall, but it is faster and easier to install and paint. The new floor was painted with a concrete sealer in a darker shade than the beige walls. This acrylic product forms a tough surface that resists stains from gasoline and oil, as well as residue from hot tires. The dropped ceiling incorporates good illumination.

This garage now features plenty of storage. In addition to a long workbench with a maple top, the durable components include wall-mounted cabinets as well as under-counter rolling cabinets. Full-extension drawers in each rolling chest are equipped with nonslip, cushioned rubber liners that keep tools securely in place. These units all feature embossed metal doors. The wall panels provide tool storage as well as a means for hanging cabinetry and shelves.

Visit Lowes.com and search with keyword "garage" to find the latest products available at Lowe's.

BEFORE This garage had become so cramped that there was no room to open car doors, let alone use the space for any kind of workstation. Aesthetically, it was too dungeon-like for the family to imagine spending any time there.

AFTER This simple but creative garage workshop makeover shows what you can do on a modest budget. After they'd cleaned the area, the homeowners painted the walls a warmer sandstone color. Then they took on the floors, taping off the car area and painting the rest light gray. To create the diamond pattern, they used a 20-inch-square piece of poster board as a pattern, chalked the outline, and filled in the shapes with a darker gray floor paint. They added storage for tools and lightweight equipment by screwing pegboard to strips of craft board that are hung from the ceiling beam. Track lighting hangs from 2 × 4s attached to an overhead beam. The work surface is a piece of ¾-inch-thick plywood resting on two five-drawer tool cabinets.

whatagreatidea

clever storage solutions
Find a way to stash all that stuff.

A garage, basement, or laundry room makeover isn't complete until you've found a place for all those things you once stacked in the corners. Consider not only how often you need to access the items but also the kind of space you have available. Lowe's has plenty of storage strategies to meet every need.

UTILIZE THE HEIGHT of the garage or basement by mounting shelving on the walls. A wire unit lets you see what's on the highest shelves without climbing a ladder. Select the most appropriate style of drawers or adjustable shelves to customize the unit for whatever items you have to store.

CEILING-MOUNTED SHELVES are ideal for large items, things you use only seasonally, and anything you're stashing for future use. Add one in a corner or run a series of shelves across an entire end of a garage or basement. Attach them securely to ceiling joists or beams.

Remodeled, a previously dungeon-like basement now invites regular use.

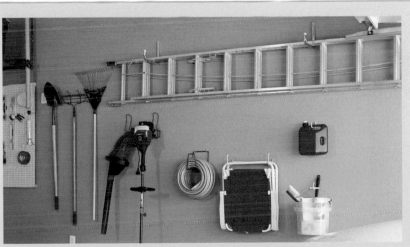

THERE ARE HOOKS AND HANGERS for almost everything. Some are designed to hang specific items, such as garden hoses, bicycles, or other sports equipment. You can screw the hooks directly into the wall or hang them from pegboard attached to furring strips.

TO KEEP THINGS out of sight and maximize floor space, install tall cabinets. Store small items in base-cabinet drawers and use the countertop as a work surface. A lockable unit hides valuables or secures pesticides and other toxic materials.

HOBBIES such as sewing, painting, flower arranging, and crafts require workspace, materials, tools, and supplies. Often you can carve out a spot for yourself at one end or corner of the garage or in a closet in your home. Here is a versatile hobby center that the whole family can enjoy.

AFTER The walls and ceiling of this once dark garage are now a warm cream color. Hooks and special hangers hold tools and sports equipment along an open stretch of wall, and pegboard (which is attached to furring strips) provides a handy place to hang lightweight craft materials. The two heights on the workbench enable all family members to use the bench comfortably and avoid back strain. Instructions for making the workbench are at right.

BEFORE An 8-foot-long area along one wall of this garage was picked as the perfect spot for a family hobby center. But first an accumulation of bikes, boxes, and other items had to be stored more efficiently. The cluttered space also needed to be made pleasant enough for hours of creativity.

multi-level workbench

You can build the bench shown on the facing page.

This workbench began with a standard plan, 48 inches long by 36 inches high by 24 inches deep. The homeowners added lower wings on the ends. In constructing the bench, think of it as front and back frames connected by cross-pieces. For every step, use a square to ensure the legs are at a 90-degree angle with the rails. Secure pieces using two deck screws.

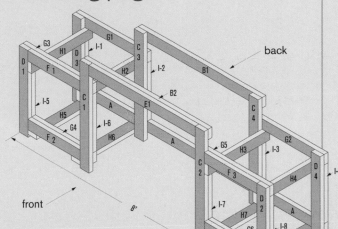

STEP 1: Cut and label all lumber according to the cut list.

STEP 2: Begin by constructing the bottom of the back frame. On bottom rail A, measure in 24 inches from each end and mark.

On end legs D3 and D4, and on middle legs C3 and C4, measure up 3 inches from one end and mark. The ends from which you measure will be the bottom of the legs. Lay out legs D3 and D4 parallel to each other on a flat surface. Position rail A on top of the legs with its bottom edge on the 3-inch marks and its ends flush with the outside edges of D3 and D4. Position legs C3 and C4 so that their outside edges are flush with the 24-inch marks on rail A. Attach each leg to the rail with two deck screws.

STEP 3: To complete the back, measure down 7 inches from the top of leg C3 and mark. Attach rail G1 between legs D3 and C3 so that its top edge is flush with the top of D3 and at the 7-inch mark on C3. Repeat this process for rail G2 and the other two legs.

Use rail B1 to connect legs C3 and C4 at the top. Attach the back leg fillers I1, I2, I3, and I4 to the back of the frame.

STEP 4: Now construct the front frame. Measure up 3 inches from one end of each of the 4 front legs (D1, D2, C1, and C2) and mark. These are the bottom ends of the legs. Position rail G4 with its bottom edge on the 3-inch marks. Attach it, screwing from the back side to keep heads from showing on the front. Repeat this step using rail G6 and legs C2 and D2.

Next, measure down 7 inches from the top of leg C1 and make a mark. Attach rail G3 between legs D1 and C1 so that its top edge is flush with the top of D1 and the 7-inch mark on C1. Attach rail G5 between legs D2 and C2 in the same manner.

Use rail B2 to connect legs C1 and C2 at the top. Finally, attach all side rail, front top rail, and front leg rail fillers to the back of the front frame.

STEP 5: To connect the front and back frames, stand them up and attach crosspieces H1 through H8 on the undersides of the rails as shown.

STEP 6: Use the plywood to create bottom shelves. Each outside corner must be notched to clear the side legs. Using a scrap piece of 2 × 4 as a template, mark the notches, approximately 3½ inches deep and 3 inches wide. Cut out the notches with a small saw; trim as necessary. Drill pilot holes and secure the two shelves with drywall screws driven into the frame.

STEP 7: Sand all rough edges. Prime and paint the base. Let the professionals at Lowe's handle ordering and installing the countertops for you. Or you can install postform countertops yourself. Lowe's will cut them to length (one at 51 inches and two at 25½ inches). Be sure to order matching caps for ends with exposed cuts. The countertops can be attached to the base with either corner brackets or figure-eight fasteners.

CUT LIST

Part	Material	Length	Quantity
A back bottom rail	2 × 4	96 inches	1
B middle rails	2 × 4	48 inches	2
C middle legs	2 × 4	36 inches	4
D end legs	2 × 4	29 inches	4
E front top rail filler	2 × 4	41 inches	1
F side rail fillers	2 × 4	20½ inches	4
G side rails	2 × 4	27½ inches	6
H crosspieces	2 × 4	24 inches	8
I leg fillers	2 × 4	19 inches	8

FRESH START

In a once-cluttered closet, a hobby haven provides organized storage for project supplies as well as a great work surface for crafts, scrapbooking, and wrapping gifts. Every square inch is maximized. On the back wall, furring strips are covered with pegboard that can be outfitted with hooks to hang almost anything. Dowels, secured to the pegboard with hooks, create an effortless system for organizing rolls of paper and ribbon. This multipurpose craft station can be hidden anytime behind the closet doors.

▲ **CLOSED CONTAINERS** A column of shelves on the right wall provides a place to store plastic storage bins, books, or other loose items.

▲ **PAPER HOLDERS** On the left side of the closet, dowels are secured to the wall at an angle, housing loose paper and gift bags. Below, dowels, installed vertically up from the floor, neatly hold long rolls of paper. For how-to instructions, visit LowesCreativeIdeas.com, click on "Archive," and select "Craft Station Organizer" under Step-by-Step Projects.

▼ **RIBBON DRAWER** Ribbons and bows will never be unravelled or lost in this customizable drawer organizer. A variety of organization items can be used to bring order to under-counter cabinets.

energy efficient by design

Remodeling your home gives you a perfect opportunity to make it more energy efficient. When you use appliances and materials that carry the ENERGY STAR® label, you can save up to 30 percent on your energy bills.

Any product that carries the ENERGY STAR label has met strict energy-efficiency criteria set by the U.S. Environmental Protection Agency. The EPA began the ENERGY STAR program in 1992, so anything in your home manufactured before then is likely to be less efficient than it could be. You can take advantage of a remodeling project to replace those older items with energy- and cost-saving ones.

Lighting

• There are many stylish lighting fixtures with the ENERGY STAR label, including torchères, ceiling-mounted and under-counter lights, wall sconces, and suspended lamps.
• Compact fluorescent light bulbs (CFLs) use 66 percent less energy than standard incandescent bulbs and last up to 10 times as long.

Fans and Air Conditioners

• Improved motors and blade designs mean that ENERGY STAR qualified ceiling fans are up to 20 percent more efficient than conventional fans.
• Ventilating fans with the ENERGY STAR label use less energy than standard models, are less noisy, and last longer.

Appliances

DISHWASHERS: A new ENERGY STAR qualified dishwasher uses 25 percent less energy than a conventional model. It contains its own water heater, so you don't have to set your main water heater temperature high just to clean your dishes.

CLOTHES WASHERS: Use 50 percent less energy and water with an ENERGY STAR qualified washer. Because it also extracts more water during the spin cycle, your clothes will dry faster.

REFRIGERATORS AND FREEZERS: Because of improved insulation, high-efficiency compressors, and better temperature controls, ENERGY STAR qualified refrigerators use about half as much energy as models manufactured before 1993.

For more information, go to Lowes.com/Energy, or ask a Lowe's employee to guide you to the most efficient products for your home remodel.

Windows, Skylights, and Doors

• Replace single-paned windows and skylights with ENERGY STAR qualified double-paned units and you will increase the comfort of your home, use your heater and air conditioner less, and protect your possessions from sun damage. Improved framing materials, glass coatings, gas fillers between the panes, and warm edge spaces account for their efficiency.

Index

Page numbers in boldface refer to photographs.

AT LOWE'S...
we're here for you!

Here are the top 10 ways in which Lowe's can help you with your home improvement endeavors.

1 Professionals install. For upgrades such as flooring, plumbing fixtures, and cabinetry, Lowe's can provide guaranteed professional installation.

2 Just ask us, and we'll order it. Take advantage of our Special Order Services. With access to more than 250,000 products, you're bound to find whatever item you're seeking.

3 We offer payment options. Choose the Lowe's Consumer Credit Card for a dedicated, revolving line of credit, to use for everyday purchases; it offers low monthly payments, no annual fee, and periodic special financing offers. For major projects, choose the Lowe's Project Card, which offers a larger line of credit to accommodate higher credit lines (up to $30,000 or more). Apply by visiting **Lowes.com** and clicking "Lowe's Credit Services" or simply drop by the store nearest you for an application.

4 We assist. We deliver, and we can provide guaranteed professional installation.

5 We guarantee our prices. Our everyday low-price guarantee eliminates comparison shopping. If we find an identical item priced lower elsewhere, we will match the price. Should we happen to miss one, we will take off an additional 10%.

6 We guarantee our plants. If a plant doesn't survive for a year after purchase, return it to your local store with the receipt, and we'll replace it.

1 YEAR GUARANTEE ON EVERY PLANT

7 Our return policy is hassle free. If you are not completely happy with your purchase, simply return it, along with your original sales receipt, to any local Lowe's store within 90 days.* We'll either repair it, replace it, refund your money, or credit your account.

*30 days for outdoor power equipment (chain saws, blowers, tillers, trimmers, mowers, and pressure washers)

8 We match your colors. Bring a sample to Lowe's, and our computers will create a matching paint shade in minutes.

9 Our experts teach you how. Check out our free How-To Clinics on every subject from installing ceramic tile to organizing storage space. For more information and to sign up, visit your local Lowe's store, or go to **Lowes.com/Clinics**.

How-To CLINICS

10 We offer friendly service. If you have any questions about a project, ask our knowledgeable staff. They'll be happy to find a solution within our store. Browse through additional projects at **Lowes.com**.